ANA BRIONGOS was born in 1946 in Barcelona, where she currently lives with her husband and two children. Ever since she first travelled to the Middle East and Asia as a student, she has been fascinated by travel. After teaching high school Physics and Mathematics for five years, and dreaming about the countries she had visited – especially Afghanistan and Iran – she applied for a scholarship to study Persian language and literature at the University of Tehrān. She worked in Iran and Afghanistan and travelled extensively through both countries.

Black on Black is Ana's first book. She has also written many articles about travel and education, and her short travel story 'A Winter in Kandahar' was awarded a special prize by the jury of the first Grandes Viajeros de Aramaio in 1998.

black on black

Iran Revisited

Ana M. Briongos
Translated by Chris Andrews

LONELY PLANET PUBLICATIONS
Melbourne • Oakland • London • Paris

Black on Black: Iran Revisited

Published by Lonely Planet Publications
    Head Office: PO Box 617, Hawthorn, Vic 3122, Australia
    Branches: 150 Linden Street, Oakland, CA 94607, USA
                  10a Spring Place, London NW5 3BH, UK
                  1 rue Dahomey, 75011, Paris, France

First published in Spanish as *Negro sobre negro: Irán, cuadernos de viaje*
(Laertes SA de Ediciones, Barcelona, 1996)
Published by Lonely Planet Publications, 2000
Printed by The Bookmaker Pty Ltd
Printed in China

Map by Tony Fankhauser
Designed by Tamsin Wilson
Edited by Janet Austin

    National Library of Australia Cataloguing in Publication Data

    Briongos, Ana M.
    [Negro sobre negro. English]
    Black on black: Iran revisited.

    Bibliography.
    ISBN 0 86442 795 6.

    1. Iran – Social conditions – 20th century.
    2. Iran – Description and travel. I. Andrews, Chris, 1962–.
    II. Title. (Series: Lonely Planet journeys.)

    955.0543

Text © Ana M. Briongos 1996, 1997
English-language translation © Christopher Stuart Andrews 2000
Map © Lonely Planet 2000

THIS book is dedicated to Bubu and Rave, with love; to Irene, who convinced me to accompany her; to Bahram who excelled in his role as Persian host; and his mother, who put me up in her house and looked after me. It is also dedicated to my old roommate, Homa.

My thanks go to Toni Catany, who was a wonderful travelling companion; to Javier Fernández de Castro, whose advice was indispensable for the completion of the book; to Francesc Casademont, who read it and commented on it; and to my family, who encouraged me to return to Iran.

Many things in the book are true, others are not, but could well have been; some of the names are fictitious as well.

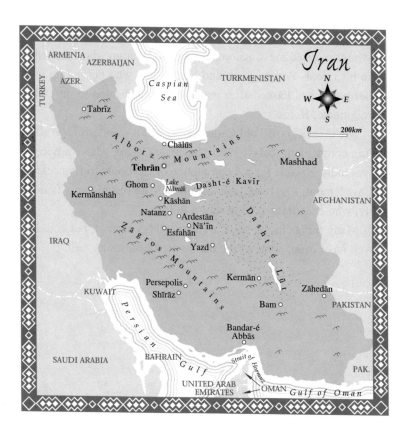

Introduction

My intention in writing this book is to give a general idea of what Iran is like today, through my comments but above all through the various characters who figure in the story. Its gentle tone does not exclude irony, but I have not ventured to judge the political situation. What has happened in Iran is complex and any denunciation from a Western point of view is bound to be simplistic and erroneous. All I have tried to do is bring the country closer to readers, offering them my vision of how Iran lives from day to day, now that the Islamic Revolutionary government seems to be firmly in place, so that they may come to their own conclusions.

31 March 1994

Tehrān – The Americans – Nō Rūz

*W*E are drinking tea around a table on which yoghurt, honey, fresh bread and soft white cheese have been laid. It's the middle of the morning and we are having breakfast after just a few hours' sleep. We arrived in Tehrān at dawn, as the muezzin was singing and the horizon turning pink.

Bahram is happy, talking and laughing. His bright smile is half-hidden by an upward-curling moustache; his skin is dark, and his prominent almond eyes flash as his hands gesticulate. Watching him, it strikes me that he could have stepped out of one of those Persian miniatures that adorn old handwritten books, and I imagine him with a turban and a damask frock coat. Hours go by as the cups are refilled, the conversation flows on, and relatives and neighbours drop in. There is no hurry at all; we are in Asia, and we have all the time in the world in front of us.

Bahram's mother welcomed us last night with the affection and easy, warm hospitality that characterise the people of this country. She seems happy now too, bringing tea from the kitchen and speaking in Fārsī with her son and Irene, who arrived with me this morning. Irene is Bahram's wife. She's Spanish, born in Barcelona like me, but she lived here in Iran with her husband and children until the war with Iraq broke out. Faced with the possibility of seeing her adolescent son conscripted, she took him and her two daughters to live with her in Barcelona. Although Bahram has visited them once or twice a year since their departure twelve years ago, Irene's return to Tehrān, after so long, is something everyone has been waiting for. Accompanying her has given me an opportunity to revisit Iran.

I am surprised by the number of Fārsī words I can remember, and find I can follow the general drift of the conversation. I learnt the language during the year I spent at the University of Tehrān's Faculty of Language and Literature, on a scholarship from the Iranian Ministry of Education. That was the 1973–74 academic year. After that, thanks to my knowledge of the country and its language, I worked for various companies and banks liaising with Iran. This involved numerous trips to Tehrān, and I spent a couple of months a year there until the situation became unstable. It was during the time of the Shāh, who gave himself the name Shāhansha, the King of Kings, and his wife, Farah Dība. The country was flooded with petrodollars, and the 2500th anniversary of the birth of the Persian Empire was celebrated with great pomp. Part of the population was growing scandalously rich and flaunting it, while the rest, the majority, lived modestly or in poverty. A powerful middle class sprang up ready to buy everything the West had to offer, and the West stepped in, handing out commissions without a thought to the consequences and giving the country a crash course in corruption. In those days Tehrān had a population of four million. Now it has twelve million.

Yesterday on the plane, an Air France flight from Paris, almost all of the passengers were Iranians; there can't have been more than six or seven foreigners. There were quite a few small children sleeping, crying or playing on the seats. Only half the women had their hair covered with scarves. The men were much more lively and garrulous than the women: smiling and waving their hands about, continuously cracking jokes, laughing and telling stories as they walked up and down the aisle. They made a great fuss over the smallest incident. During the flight some of them ordered whisky, and others drank wine with their meal. This trip was a homecoming for them, a return to family comforts. They were leaving behind a world that was not theirs, a difficult and often hostile world. The video screens showed our position on a map, and the path traced by the aircraft since our departure from Paris. As we passed over Tabrīz, the first major city in Iran after crossing the border with Turkey, the air hostess announced that alcoholic beverages would no longer be served, and instructed passengers to hand in any alcohol they might have left, as well as empty bottles and lids. Every trace had to be eliminated.

One by one the women who had been travelling bareheaded covered themselves, and on arrival in Tehrān, all of us, without exception, had our overgarments on and our headscarves in place. Even the French air hostesses.

Going through customs was easy: the officials were friendly and I didn't see anyone who had to open their suitcase to have it checked. The only question repeated with a certain insistence was: "Are you carrying a video camera?" If you answered no, you went through. They weren't interested in ordinary cameras, or at all suspicious of them. Toni Catany, a professional photographer travelling with us, was burdened with his cameras and spools of film, but they didn't want to see what he was carrying when he said no to the question about the video camera. A couple of days later at the state tourism office, where we had gone to look at maps and check out the details of our trip, they asked us the same question again, but wouldn't tell us why it was so important. No-one could give us a logical explanation, nor have we heard one since.

The airport's third-world appearance surprised me. I remembered a modern building, but couldn't recognise anything at all. It was as if I had never been there before, although of course I had, having arrived and departed more than twenty times between 1973 and 1977. I had also very nearly witnessed the collapse of the main building's roof – a national catastrophe – and seen it rebuilt, twenty years ago now.

On that occasion, I'd escaped with my life thanks to a blond adventurer I'd met at the Spanish embassy two days before I was due to go home. We had both come to pick up our mail. It was the first time we had seen each other, but when our eyes met, there was electricity. The next day, it so happened that he was passing by the university gate just as several trucks full of impeccably equipped policemen arrived to enforce a brutal crackdown. He recognised me as a mob of students swarmed around us, and took me by the hand. Without a word being said, I found myself on the other side of Avenue Shāh Rezā, my back against the wall, his back pressed against my nose. Then he dragged me away with a jolt, and we went running through the backstreets and alleys until the sound of the megaphone barking orders and threats faded away. The amplified tones weren't those of the muezzins calling the faithful to kneel facing Mecca; they were shouts of anger. Who could have known that the end of an empire was so near at hand?

A street vendor offered us tinned sardines from Galicia, and leaning against his grimy stand we savoured them on the spot, along with a *nān*, Iranian flat bread, still warm from the oven of the bakery across the way. The food tasted good, and the electricity between us was still there. We could only laugh at the situation we found ourselves in. The blond turned out to be a sailor and traveller from Asturias, in northern Spain. We spoke the same language, and after so much time away from home it was comforting to be able to lose myself in conversation with someone who shared my reactions to the stimuli of Tehrān. With his hand warm in mine once again it was clear that this wasn't going to end tomorrow. We didn't know each other, or what we were doing so far away from home, but if the stars had agreed to make our paths cross twice, how could we let the opportunity pass us by? Destiny had insisted on bringing us together. That afternoon we went to change my plane ticket. I would have been crazy not to spend an extra week in Tehrān with that man whose eyes were like two seas.

The first snow had not yet fallen on the peaks of the Alborz mountains, and at their feet the sun-baked streets were giving off that smell of poorly refined petrol so characteristic of Middle Eastern cities.

The next day, the catastrophe was in the news: the roof of Tehrān's airport had fallen in. Dozens of dead bodies had been found in the rubble, and I wasn't among them because a stranger had taken me by the hand on Avenue Shāh Rezā and pulled me from the whirlpool. *Allāho Akbar, Allāho Akbar –* God is Great – kept resounding in my head. Everyone seemed to agree, brothers all, united in their struggle against the same demon. North of Shāh Rezā, the providential stranger and I celebrated with kisses. North of Shāh Rezā, where the men wore diamond rings and the women in Christian Dior dresses had doctorates from the Sorbonne or PhDs from Stanford.

13

South of Shāh Rezā, the swarming streets and lanes, the bazaar, women wearing the *chādor*; simple, ordinary, devout people, still untouched by corruption and bribery. The south of Tehrān, where the Revolution was brewing, in mosques and in gyms full of massive weightlifters, where the mullahs were in control, where Ramadan was strictly observed, where no alcohol or pork were consumed, where we loved to wander, day after day. From the window of our refuge in the north of the city we could see Karīm Khān-é Zand Avenue and the Armenian cathedral on the corner.

My first impression on leaving the airport this time, at the end of the night, with dawn about to break and the muezzin's prayer sounding, is that the cars parked outside are very old and decrepit: clapped-out Renaults and Iranian-made Paykans with rusty panels. They must have been on the road the last time I came here. The big cars have gone, and now you don't even see any old, run-down ones. Not a single American make, just the occasional antiquated Mercedes like the one belonging to my host, Bahram – the newest and best-preserved vehicle to be seen, and it's a '78 model! I ask about the Paykans and am told they're still being made, but I can't see any new ones as we turn into what used to be known as Eisenhower Avenue (though now of course it has another name) and advance into the immense city of Tehrān. The conundrum remains: where are the new Paykans?

The street names have changed; like the flag, the coins and the paper money.

During the flight I was thinking of my first arrival in Tehrān by plane, clutching the letter from the Iranian Ministry of Education notifying me that I had been granted a scholarship, and the telegram confirming that someone would be waiting for me at the airport.

Before that, I had passed through Tehrān three times, but neither the country nor the city had interested me at the time because I had been in search of the promised land. Not just for me, but for many young people around the world, the promised land was Afghanistan, on the way to India and Nepal. I first came into contact with Iran in the late 1960s, a year after the Six Day War and a few months after France's May '68. I arrived in Tehrān on a coach from Baghdad, having crossed Lebanon, Syria, Jordan and Iraq, always in coaches full of men, women, children, chickens and, as I found out when I got to Tehrān, fleas. Repeatedly, during the various legs of the trip, patrols armed with machine guns would climb aboard, tripping over the chickens and slipping on the orange peel and date stones strewn over the floor of the coach. The tension of the Six Day War was still in the air, and the searches were rigorous. I stayed just three or four days in Tehrān, long enough to get the visa that would allow me to enter Afghanistan. In those days, travelling in the region with a Spanish passport was a delight. Spanish citizens didn't need a visa for Iran, nor for Lebanon, Syria, Jordan or Iraq. Spain was considered a friendly country: it had not taken part in the colonisation of the region, nor in the division of the spoils after the First World War, and it did not maintain diplomatic relations with Israel. There were also many Arab students in the medical faculties in Spain, and just about everyone had a relative or an acquaintance who was studying in Zaragoza. I stayed opposite the train station, where there was a series of cheap hotels frequented by young travellers on their way east. And the train took me to the eastern border of Iran.

The second time, some months later, I arrived on a coach again, but this time I had crossed Turkey: Istanbul, Trabzon, Erzurum, Tabrīz, Tehrān. A day in the city to get the Afghan visa, then a coach to Mashhad, on the north-eastern border of Iran. I was twenty, travelling on my own, and I never had any problems. I had deferred my course at the Faculty of Physics in Barcelona, with its classes, pracs and exams, to immerse myself in the permanent university of travelling through other countries and getting to know their people. It isn't just the forests, the seas, the rivers, the deserts, the paths and the daybreaks that teach you things; it isn't just the monuments and the museums: it's also the men, the women and the children who live by those paths and in those deserts. It's important to travel when you're young: you travel light and cheap, and your heart is like a sponge. The paths across the world make up a school which tempers the character and reinforces tolerance and solidarity. You learn to give and take, to keep the doors open in the house of the spirit, and above all to share. You learn to enjoy small things, to value what you have, to be happy in times of scarcity and to celebrate abundance. You learn to listen, to watch, and to love. Young people from wealthy countries should all spend a year of their lives, before family and work obligations tie them down forever, travelling around the world, from city to city, from village to village, with a pack on their backs. They'd lose a year in the race for success – but what's a year? – and they would gain personally, because it would open their horizons, which are often limited to chasing marks in an exam, and the world would be a better place.

In 1970, the third time I passed through Tehrān, I was heading for Kabul in a cream Renault Gordini, which was already a museum piece and caused a sensation among the travellers who crossed its path. The Gordini belonged to a student at the Autonomous University of Barcelona, Joan Rovira from Terrassa, and only he could drive it because the gears had been chewed up and you had to know them intimately. As well as Joan, there was Josep Ramoneda, now a journalist, my brother Miguel, and me. Joan drove all those thousands of kilometres without relief. We put wet towels on the back of his neck when it got stiff, and when night was falling and there were just a few dozen kilometres left to go to the destination we had decided on, we had to keep yelling: "Right, go right!", "Left, to the left!" and "Watch out for the sheep!" because by that stage it was all a blur for him. We had a blue tent with a single centre pole, Apache style, which we used for shelter and also to spread over the mattresses to cover the stains on the sheets of indeterminate colour waiting for us in dirt-cheap hotels. In Tehrān, we stayed on the outskirts of the city in a camping ground that I have never been able to find again. The only thing I remember is that we had to go under a bridge to get there. As we went under it, the cream Gordini got caught between a car with flat tyres and sparking rims trying to get away from the police, and a patrol car, from which someone was yelling incomprehensible sentences through a megaphone while policemen leant out of the windows spraying gunshots around. The phantom car, enveloped in sparks, went off the road as soon as it got out from under the bridge and raised such a cloud of dust that it managed to lose the police and was never seen again. We went on to the camping ground, checking ourselves and each other to make sure there weren't any holes anywhere.

Later still I flew over Tehrān in a plane belonging to the indescribable Ariana Afghan Airlines, a plane without seats, in which the passengers sat on their sleeping bags on the floor, if they weren't among the blessed who were able to sleep inside them.

A woman travelling on her own has to know how to look after herself and be respected, which means dressing appropriately and using common sense. Travelling on her own, a woman has access to places where a man could never go. During those trips to Afghanistan I lived with the women of a Baluchi tribe, camped near Herat, was taken in by the women and children of a judge in Kandahar, shared the tents and the work of Hazara tribeswomen in Band-i-Amir, lived with the Cuchis of Bamiyan, wearing a beautiful red dress (which I still have) made of hundreds of pieces of cloth and weighed down with glass beads, and in Maymaneh I stayed with the wives of the men who breed the horses for *buzkashi*, the Afghan national sport. I was so fascinated by Afghanistan that I felt compelled to learn its language, Persian, which is called Darí in Afghanistan and Fārsī in Iran. But who was going to give me a scholarship to study Persian? Obviously not Afghanistan. The country was so poor it didn't even figure in the list of developing nations. Iran would give me a scholarship if I applied for one; so I did. In those days Iran was a rich country, riding on the petrol boom. I was awarded a postgraduate scholarship to do a doctorate in Persian language and literature at the University of Tehrān. Since I already had a degree in physics, the next step was a doctorate. I couldn't get through to them that I would be starting with the alphabet. Take it or leave it. I took it.

Although I had been there more often than I'd been to Madrid, Tehrān didn't really exist for me until the night I arrived with the letter from the Ministry. Looking down from a plane wrapped in darkness, I saw the city spread out below me like an immense carpet strewn with stars.

Nobody was waiting for me, in spite of the telegram. I had feared as much, because I was getting to know how things worked in that part of the world. Later on, of course, I was told they couldn't find me. During the flight I had been talking with some French television reporters who were toting bulky camera equipment, and when they saw me standing there alone and helpless at midnight, with no-one to meet me, they took pity on me and kindly dropped me off at a simple but decent hotel, the Hotel America, in front of the United States embassy. Wherever you go in the world there is solidarity among travellers. You can rely on it.

From the balcony of my room I could just see over the high wall surrounding the embassy gardens on the other side of Tahté-Jamshid Avenue: this was the first view I had in my year in Tehrān. Years later, at the beginning of the Revolution, the embassy would be the scene of the terrible hostage crisis, which went on for months and months, four hundred and forty-four days exactly. Standing on that balcony, taking my first look at the streets of Tehrān, how could I have guessed that it would later be the vantage point used by television crews from around the world to film the embassy when it was occupied by the guerrilla fighters of the Revolution.

Among the guests in the Hotel America was Mr Khalili, correspondent for the Egyptian newspaper *Al-Ahram*, a man with totally white hair. He was the first person I met in Tehrān and he took me under his wing during the two days I spent trying to get in touch with the Ministry of Education. He was a kind man.

When I arrived in '73, the tentacles of Amriká, as the Iranians say, held the country in a firm grasp. It was no coincidence that the United States ambassador had held one of the top jobs in the CIA before being posted to Tehrān.

During my stay I met two people who gave me an idea of how America operated in Iran: Peter and Mandy. Peter was a curious individual. I met him in a taxi. He was American, red-headed, lame and slightly hunched, a talkative stickybeak, a true adventurer and a drunk (I once gave him a bottle of Fundador which had been passed on to me by a friend of a friend who had come from Spain). He worked as a photographer for *National Geographic*, and he told me that his company, the biggest in the United States so he said, had more than thirty people working in Iran, making maps for the Iranian army and, incidentally, for the CIA. To keep up appearances, he did the odd story with pretty photos for the magazine. Peter had short greasy hair full of dandruff, bags under his eyes and a two-day stubble, and he got around in a worn-out brown corduroy suit. He knew everyone in Tehrān, and moved through the city like a slippery eel. He didn't miss a trick: soon after I arrived, he managed to get into the same taxi as me and, true to form, exploited the opportunity to find out who this lost-looking girl sitting next to him was, and what she was doing in Tehrān. From that day on he dropped by the residential college where I was staying at least once a month. He would invite me to dinner in some dive that smelt like bad plumbing and tell me about all the spy movies that were happening for real at that very moment in Tehrān. I found his stories entertaining, and no doubt listened to them wide-eyed, with my mouth hanging open.

And then there was Mandy, the only American student in

my class at the University of Tehrān. Mandy was very blonde, a bit like a Barbie doll. She was the only one in the class who had a flat and a car, a yellow two-seater Honda convertible that she drove to university. Mandy was a Mormon, from Salt Lake City; she played bridge, and when I knew her she was working as a secretary for the Iranian Minister of Foreign Affairs. Every morning, a car picked her up and took her to the Ministry. She came to classes when she could. She didn't mix with the other students, but every once in a while she would ask me out to the cinema or for a drink in the restaurant of some luxury hotel which she didn't want to visit on her own. I liked riding in a yellow two-seater convertible through the streets of Tehrān. That car really was a quite a sight, especially with Mandy in it and her long blonde hair blowing in the wind. Mandy was looking for a husband. Back in the United States she had finished a Master's in international politics, and now it was time for her to find the right man. But in spite of everything she had going for her, she only managed to attract very young, handsome but poor Iranian boys, the sort who work as lifesavers at the pool in the Hilton. What these boys wanted was to marry a rich American who would take them to the United States. Unfortunately, Mandy wasn't really rich; she was just an American with a well-paid job, who liked to show off.

Mandy always needed someone to keep her company and to sort out the little problems of her daily life, and while the life-saver she happened to have in tow performed these functions, he unfortunately also kept away potential husbands. That was where I came in. To tell the truth, the times I went out with her we didn't meet anyone; not one filthy-rich prince charming came anywhere near us. But the lifesaver did, every day: he

21

would be waiting for her in the street when she came back from work in the official car. He took her suits to the dry-cleaner's, did the shopping, unblocked her drains and I don't know what else. The only one of these hopefuls I got to know, Abbas, was a good sort: extremely handsome, tall, strong and healthy, always ready to sort out whatever problem came up. Yet in spite of his affectionate and pleasant nature, he suffered from monumental attacks of jealousy when he found out that Mandy was going out with someone else, and kicked up such a fuss that soon the whole neighbourhood knew about it. For Mandy the problem was how to get rid of him when things started getting ugly. He talked to me as if we were both on the same side, and in fact we were. In the end what both of us were doing with Mandy was practising our English. Once, though, I saw him cry.

One day Mandy told me she had received a letter proposing that she work for the CIA. I was so naïve. Mandy didn't strike me as being in the least suited for that sort of work, but before I could burst out laughing and make some humorous comment about the CIA and the Americans, she said:

"I'm thinking about doing it, because the States needs normal, liberal-minded citizens to do these jobs and not just the crazies they usually get."

I was dumbstruck. Obviously Mandy was a valuable person for the CIA, with her job in the Iranian Ministry of Foreign Affairs. From that moment, my perception of her changed. At first she had struck me as a frivolous and slightly scatter-brained girl, obsessed with vitamins (she explained to me what 'complexion' meant), but from then on, I saw her as an American, a Republican and a Mormon, first and foremost.

Today, the 31st of March, our first day in Iran, we went for a drive to Darband, in the north of the city. Darband is a street that runs between walls of rock, following the valley of a stream towards the Alborz mountains, in whose foothills Tehrān is nestled. It is the starting point for walking trails into the mountains, and on Fridays it's busy with hikers and strollers. There are decks straddling the stream on which you can sit and drink tea while looking down over the city or up at the snow on the peaks, enjoying the calm atmosphere, the cool air wafting off the nearby mountains and the murmur of the water flowing all around. It's a spectacular climb up the old Pahlavī Avenue, lined with tall, leafy plane trees, the Alborz mountains and their highest peak, the colossal snow-covered Damāvand, rearing up ahead and blocking the way. The inhabitants of Tehrān swear that it's the longest avenue in the world. In over thirty kilometres, it sees the city rise from an altitude of a thousand metres in the south to eighteen hundred metres at its northern extremity. Abundant, clear water from melting snow and ice can be seen flowing along both sides of the avenue, lapping at the foot of the trees. The water flows through the northern part of Tehrān in the *jūbs*, as the channels on either side of the street are called. By the time it reaches the south, it is already dirty, thick and brown. The south is where the poor live: the disinherited and the *mostazafīn*, the people Khomeinī's speeches were aimed at.

I have seen the south of Tehrān. I saw it when I delivered two suitcases full of clothes that Mandy had left for Abbas and his family when she went back to the United States. Since she hadn't left me the telephone number – later I found out that there wasn't a phone in the house – I decided to take the suitcases to them myself. It was a long drive in the taxi. As we

23

went south from Avenue Shāh Rezā, now Avenue of the Revolution, the surroundings became less pleasant and the poverty more obvious: first ramshackle houses, then little brick cubicles, more or less weatherproof, and finally huts made of wood, tin and asbestos. The taxi dropped me off in a bog, and as I got out I put my foot straight into a foul-smelling puddle. Then I had to find Abbas's house. Guided by a herd of ragged children milling all around me, I set off stumbling and weaving through piles of rubbish, burdened with the two suit-cases. Groups of youths on street corners stared at me absently; women with their *chādor*s hitched up went by carry-ing buckets full of dun-coloured water.

Finally I found Abbas, sitting on a stone shaped like a bench, drawing in the dirt in front of his house with a stick. It was a Friday afternoon, the Muslim festive day, so he didn't have to work. I sat down beside him on that stone, and he told me that he had six little brothers and sisters, that his father was dead, and that it was lucky he had a good job. Lots of the men in the neighbourhood didn't have jobs; they survived by sell-ing smuggled tobacco, making deliveries and licking the boots of the rich people in the north. The young ones killed their hunger with heroin and turned to dealing. They were the chil-dren of farmers who had come to the city in their thousands, wave after wave of them, chasing the mirage of industrial development and driven by the impoverished state of rural Iran, neglected by the Pahlavī dynasty. I remembered that I had seen Abbas cry one day at Mandy's house. Those tears were the tears of the powerless.

You could say that the whole of Tehrān was a factory: in the east, there was the big refinery manufacturing petrol products; in the west, the motor works turning out cars and trucks; the north was fabricating dreams; while the south was a factory producing hate.

Abbas was ill at ease, and didn't like me seeing where he lived. He thanked me for having brought him the suitcases, but I could tell straight away from the expression on his face when he recognised me that he would have preferred me not to come. He asked me not to tell anyone about my visit to that part of town, because the people from the north wouldn't understand. For them, the south didn't exist. But the south did exist, I had seen it with my own eyes, and it was a huge bomb about to explode.

When the Revolution came, they changed the name of Pahlavī Avenue to Mosadeq. Mosadeq – the hero, the patriot, the legend, the man who got Iran's petrol back, perhaps the country's most important politician in modern times, ousted by the CIA in order to put the Shāh back on the throne in 1953. At the beginning of the Revolution they gave his name to Tehrān's most important avenue, which until then had been called after the Imperial family. But the new name didn't last long. Mosadeq was the hero of the secular liberals, who enthusiastically got behind the Revolution, alongside the Islamic clergy, to put in place a new Iran without a monarchy, but they too were soon swept aside, imprisoned, assassinated, obliged to flee the country or condemned to ostracism within it. Khomeinī didn't like Mosadeq, although he could be used as an anti-American symbol, and his name was expunged from the street signs just a few months after it had appeared. Now the avenue is called Valī-yé Asr, which means the Prince of this Time; that is, the Twelfth Emām, the hidden, hoped-for one, who is to come.

At the foot of the mountains we buy *albalūs* – a red acidic fruit, round like peas – boiled broad beans and walnuts softened in brine. In front of us there is a huge painted concrete sculpture representing a guardian of the Revolution in military dress. Children are climbing up onto its arms to have their photos taken. We polish off the broad beans, *albalūs* and walnuts, and stroll back towards the city, refreshed along the way by rich ice cream flavoured with rose-water.

Since leaving the house this morning, Irene and I have been wearing the Islamic uniform for women: a light overcoat, and a headscarf known as a *rūsārī*. I'm well aware that my beige coat doesn't cover my ankles, and am worried that this detail will give me away as a foreigner. What's more, these coats are not normally beige; almost all of them are dark grey or black.

We have reached Ferdōsī Avenue, which, like the square to which it leads, hasn't had to undergo a name change because it is called after the great Persian poet. I remembered it being full of shops, hundreds of them, with carpets stacked up to the roof. I used to come here after classes, and ended up getting to know quite a few dealers, with whom I would spend the afternoons drinking tea. The transactions would continue, accompanied by a ritual display: carpets unfolded one on top of the other until the pile was waist-high, then one by one folded up again and put away. I would leave those shops with my head spinning. I learnt how to recognise the Tabrīz carpets, with their characteristic pistachio-green colour; the ones from Ghom, each square a little landscape with animals and weeping willows; those from Esfahān, with a sky-blue background; or from Nā'īn or Kermān, and many other varieties.

Now there's not a single shop left. There seems to be lots of empty warehouses, and not a trace of that flourishing commerce. It's true that many businesses are still closed for the Nō Rūz holiday, the Persian New Year, celebrated around the 21st of March to coincide with the spring equinox. In Fārsī, Nō Rūz means 'New Day'; it's part of the Zoroastrian heritage, and the most important non-Islamic festival in the Iranian year. More than eight thousand years ago, the Zoroastrian calendar had already singled out four feast days initiating the year's four seasons. The most important marked the beginning of spring. According to archaeologists, it was so important that the great palace of Persepolis was built specifically to house the Persian king's celebration of the festival. He received ambassadors, dignitaries and tribal emissaries who came to bring him tributes. Afterwards the palace stood empty, guarded only by a few warriors throughout the year, until the king came back to celebrate the next Nō Rūz.

Originally, the festival lasted for forty days, and involved visits, music, dances and games. Everyone enjoyed themselves, except for those in mourning, and taxes were not collected. Now it lasts thirteen days. The festivities begin on *chahārshambé-yé-surī*, the last Wednesday before New Year. On that day, bonfires are lit in the streets, and people jump over them to secure their happiness during the coming year. It is rumoured that the mullahs want to eliminate the festival, by bringing it forward to coincide with the anniversary of the Revolution. But the tradition of Nō Rūz runs so deep among the people that this year there were more bonfires than ever, and everyone, however unsprightly, was trying to jump over them. Years ago, the then prime minister Hoveīda jumped over one: I saw it on television and on the front page of the newspapers. And amid laughter and shoving, I jumped over the bonfire that had been built in a corner of the university,

27

along with the other girls from the residential college. Obviously we were wearing jeans and being rather daring. It wouldn't have occurred to me then to wonder what changes were coming, though soon enough I began to realise that the Iran a visitor saw on arrival was covered with a veneer of Western modernity, which you only had to scratch to find the authentic Iran, rock solid beneath. That much was clear from a number of premonitory incidents. One occurred in our residential college.

The hundred or so girls who during the academic year lived in that modern, well-appointed, five-storey building, with double rooms, plenty of baths and showers, a fridge on each floor, lifts, an intercom, kitchens, dining rooms etc., were all Iranians from the provinces with three exceptions, including me. The three of us were over twenty-three, we were all doing doctorates in Persian Language and Literature, and we were often invited to dinners and receptions at embassies or within the university, by professors, many of whom were married to foreign women, or by families of mixed origins. At that time in Tehrān the Westernised families who had sent their children abroad to study kept up a busy social life. The newly arrived female graduate student was inundated with invitations and overwhelmed everywhere she went by the warm welcome foreigners are given in Iran, but it was partly because she was a possible wife for a son or a friend with a good job who was still unmarried or divorced.

Professional Iranian men who had studied in Europe or North America liked to marry educated foreign women. Partly because of the prestige it brought them and partly because, in principle, they were less trouble than Iranian women, so everyone said. The typical foreign wife was once a normal girl, working in London or Berlin as an au pair or secretary, or simply studying at university. One day she met an Iranian man. He was rich, affectionate and alone in a foreign country, and she fell hopelessly in love with him, not thinking that the man she had known in London would not be the same when he took her back to Iran to be his wife, and resumed his place in what was inevitably a large and tightly structured family. To make it work, she had to fall in love with the country and its ways as well.

Irene fell in love with Bahram in London, and with Iran when she got married and went to live there. You only have to see her, surrounded by her husband's family, to realise that the country has become an essential part of who she is. Her vision of Iran – intelligent, sympathetic yet incisive – is a vision still informed by love.

Iranian women, if they were beautiful and came from a good family, could demand a sizeable *mahr* from their future husband, and this was set down in the *gabaleh*, or marriage contract. The *mahr* can consist of money, houses, gardens, jewels or other items of property; the husband must hand these over to his wife if he initiates divorce proceedings, but not if it happens the other way round. It's a way of protecting Muslim women: in Iran, the inability to have children, or male children, is a frequent cause of divorce. But Iranian women had, and still have for that matter, formidable mothers, imposing fathers and mobs of brothers, uncles, cousins, second cousins and other relatives to back them up and keep the husband in line.

Foreign women just got married. They didn't ask for anything, and in most cases, they didn't know they could. Nor did they have large, well-organised families behind them.

In the residential college where I lived, there were some girls who always put on an overgarment and headscarf when they went out, but most wore Western clothes without the *chādor*. In the beginning, I assumed that the girls with the headscarves were country girls hanging on to their old customs, and I didn't give it a second thought. After a while, I began to notice that they got together in one another's rooms and formed a more or less cohesive group. One day they called a meeting, put up posters on all the floors, and asked the rector and other administrators to attend. Some said it was about going out at night, because only the three foreign students had permission to stay out later than nine. I thought the idea was to demand the same rights for the Iranian students, because up until then, in my experience as a student activist in Barcelona, meetings were all about demanding and obtaining more freedom and more rights. I didn't go to the meeting, but you can imagine how surprised I was when I was told that the girls with the headscarves had asked the authorities to prevent any resident from leaving or returning to the college after nine, because the establishment had to maintain its good reputation. From that day on, the doors of the college shut at nine without exception, and I and the other foreign students either got back in time or simply had to notify the rector – a woman who had studied at the Sorbonne and wore Christian Dior suits – letting her know that we wouldn't be back until the next day. I never had any trouble with the girls in headscarves, they greeted me in a friendly enough fashion, but I never got close to any of them either. They were demure, reserved and good students, or so it seemed. I tended to attract the girls who were interested in politics and sympathetic to the communist Tūdeh party; they discussed García Lorca's poems with me and told me about their impossible love affairs. In Spain, Franco was still alive; here, the Shāh's police checked identity cards at the university gate just like the Generalísimo's men at the gates of the University of Barcelona.

On Ferdōsī Avenue there are men with calculators at the ready, attaché cases and wads of bills, changing foreign money. One dollar, two hundred and fifteen *tōmāns*, we were told during our walk today. Multiplied by ten that makes over two thousand *rials* in normal Iranian currency. Prices are usually given in *tōmāns*, but until you get used to it you're never sure that you're not being quoted a price in *rials*. There are two solutions. You can either ask straight out what the unit of currency is, which marks you as someone unfamiliar with the country or the money, or you can use your reason: if what you're buying seems expensive, it's in *rials*; if it seems very cheap, it's in *tōmāns*, in which case you have to multiply by ten to get the real price, because the bills used for buying and selling are all in denominations of *rials*. It's like talking about dimes and dollars. The problem is that they never say either *rial* or *tōmān*, because the price is a number, just a number, and you have to work it out for yourself.

The wads of bills are a visible sign of the inflation besetting Iran. Everything costs a wad.

I think I'll come back to Ferdōsī after the Nō Rūz holiday to see what the atmosphere's like on a working day.

I have the impression that there are no foreigners about, or if there are, they have opted for the chameleon-like strategy of making themselves look as much like Iranians as possible, so

31

as not to stand out. This seems an excellent idea, especially for me: being a woman and having dark eyes are advantages for travelling incognito through Iran. But I'll have to work on my Muslim uniform. I have seen lots of overgarments and head-scarves, but fewer *chādor*s. Nevertheless, all the women, without exception, are completely covered up, and it's hot. What must it be like in summer?

In a restaurant we ate *chelō kabāb* (white rice with pieces of grilled lamb), yoghurt with *sabzī* (raw greens) and soft white cheese, and we drank not Pepsi or Coca but *Parsi* Cola. Throughout the meal we kept our overgarments and head-scarves on, like all the other women.

To me, the city looks clean though run-down like it always did, but Irene thinks it looks more run-down than before.

Back at the house, it's nearly nine o'clock and visitors have started to arrive: they have come to pay their respects to Irene, the wife just back from twelve years spent abroad. I can hear the laughter and talking from my room, and imagine they are sitting around the table drinking tea. When I go out to meet them, they all introduce themselves warmly and ceremoni-ously, and the lively gathering continues. There is a knock at the door and a young couple appear with two small children. The little girl, about five years old, slim, dark and delicate, is wearing a dress of shiny pink satin and tulle, and holding pink and white gladioli. She looks like a little princess from a fairy tale. I am touched by her expression as she gives the flowers to Irene. In that instant everything stands still: a second of silence, and then the laughter resumes.

Dinner consists of soup and bread with soft white cheese and *sabzī*. They say that if a woman prepares flat bread, cheese and herbs, all rolled up together in traditional Iranian fashion, and gives it to her boyfriend or husband, he won't go off with other women. It's an old saying.

The mother of the little pink gladioli-bearing princess kisses and hugs Bahram's mother, who smiles happily and explains to me that this is her adopted daughter, who was orphaned when she was a young child. The woman has kept her overgarment and headscarf on right through the meal, in spite of the fact that she is in her mother's house. Over dessert we talk about Khomeinī and the Shāh. They don't seem to be very critical of the Revolution: some things have been done badly, they say, but there have been many positive changes as well. Bahram's mother tells us that in a couple of day's time she will be going to Mashhad to teach as a volunteer for a few weeks in a school for war orphans. She is a secondary maths teacher, retired now. Each year she spends a few weeks doing this voluntary work, more out of goodwill than devotion to a cause. She is religious without making a show of it, and since she receives a small pension, owns her house and is in good health, she is in a position to do something for the community. She studied mathematics in Iran, and speaks only Fārsī. Talking with her, I get the impression that she is at ease in her role as an Iranian woman; she lives modestly and is independent.

Tomorrow we're leaving for the Caspian sea, where we'll spend the last two days of the break. We'll be taking blankets with us, because they say it's cold up there.

1 April

On the way to the Caspian Sea

*J*AM in Chālūs, right on the Caspian Sea. We left Tehrān at dawn: the muezzin was calling and Bahram's mother was saying the day's first prayers. We headed north, and by the time we got out of the city, the day had well and truly begun. Because there was almost no traffic, it took us only three quarters of an hour to get through the enormous, completely new suburbs full of high-rise buildings which have sprung up on the outskirts and been attached to the city by means of overpasses and underpasses. I realised just how much Tehrān has grown over the last few years.

We began the ascent into the Alborz mountains, with the Caspian sea waiting for us behind them. We crossed narrow ravines, following the River Karaj, and climbed to four thousand metres among snow-covered peaks. The road was almost empty, because of the holiday. The sunshine was brilliant and it was hot. The trees on the south side of the range had begun to sense the approach of spring, and though still bare, were hinting at the colours of their leaves to come. The stones were light green, the same colour as many of the houses in the area.

As soon as we crossed the divide, the weather changed: the sky grew overcast, there was a moist smell and it was cool, almost cold. On the north side, the trees hadn't yet woken from their hibernation and were still in winter dress, but as we descended the slopes, we gradually entered a lush and humid Persia, totally different from the country on the other side of the mountains. In the old days, the caravans took four or five days to cover the hundred and thirty kilometres separating Tehrān from the Caspian. Today it took us four hours by car, which is a lot these days for such a short distance.

The villages on the coast are packed with people because it's the weekend. There are little houses and gardens everywhere you look. The climate is subtropical and the vegetation abundant: forests, fruit trees and palm trees. Here on the plain, beside the sea, springtime comes later than in the Mediterranean and you can hardly make out the colours of the leaves on the trees, which, along with the grey shades of the mist and the overcast sky, give the landscape a pastel look. It's drizzling and the ground is muddy; cows are grazing, and the villages are hives of activity. The cars don't look as old as those I saw in Tehrān, and it strikes me that this could be the reason for my impression on that first day: the only people left in the capital were the poor, with their run-down cars.

I remember that during the Nō Rūz of 1974, when I was a student at the University of Tehrān, the residential college was deserted. Many girls went back to their villages, but many also took advantage of the holidays to have nose operations. For Persian men, a big nose is a source of pride, whereas Persian women are proud of their small, perfect noses, often the products of surgery. In those days, a great number of highly qualified plastic surgeons had clinics in Iran. I suppose many of them left the country when the Revolution came, like thousands of other professionals, but I'm sure they will return, if they are not already doing so. There will always be work for them.

A patrol stopped us on the road, a simple formality, and the guard, a young man with a beard – tall, strong, good-looking and impeccably kitted out – delivered a little sermon for the benefit of the women in the car, with our overgarments and *rūsārīs*; it sounded like a poem being recited (the Persian language has that effect), and was all about the special care Muslim women must take among the perversions of the holiday towns to the north. At the end, he excused himself very respectfully and wished us a good trip. I was surprised by the gentle tone of his speech, coming from a guard of the Revolution. It was like a word of warning among believers. Because we are travelling in a car with an Iranian number plate and an Iranian driver, no-one realises we are foreigners.

We are in a house full of people, and more keep arriving, men and women of all ages. The only one wearing a headscarf indoors is the eighty-year-old grandmother. The other women have make-up on, and their hair is dyed. It looks to me like any group of friends and relatives spending the holidays together, eating, drinking and playing cards. The house is modern and comfortable, half beach house, half chalet, with lots of wood and a fire burning in the hearth.

It's still drizzling outside.

2 April

Chālūs – Caspian Sea

*F*OUR of us slept in the one room, with mattresses on the floor and blankets. When I got up early, a card game was still going on in the attic. In the lounge there were people sleeping on the sofas and on the carpet, wrapped in blankets; an elderly couple were having breakfast at a table in front of the window. It was still raining and you couldn't see more than a few dozen metres in the fog. There's supposed to be a view of beautiful mountains and dense forests, but I still haven't seen it. Next to the chimney, the opium pipe, the tongs, the burnt coals and that unmistakable acrid smell – remains of the night before; in a corner of the American-style kitchen, a demijohn of vodka bought on the sly from some home still. The Revolutionary guard did warn us.

Tomorrow is the thirteenth day since Nō Rūz, the last feast day of the New Year. We're going shopping at the local village market to prepare a big meal. We put our Muslim uniforms on over what we wear around the house before going out into the garden. It's actually convenient not to have to think about what to wear and how to do your hair before going out: you put on your overgarment or your *chādor*, which covers everything, and off you go!

We buy beautifully fresh fish in a large, clean shop. Fish is sold by auction, with men doing the bidding, six or seven at once, each with a bundle of notes in his hand. In the back of the shop, they open a sturgeon for us and fill up the saucepan we have brought with eggs. This is an illegal sale, because sturgeon fishing and the caviar industry are state monopolies.

We have fun in the fruit and vegetable market buying all sorts of herbs, preserves and sauces for cooking. The women who work in this market wear their *chādor*s hitched up a bit and are chatty to the point of cheekiness. The dealing is done in a relaxed and happy atmosphere. They let us taste various brews from big wooden spoons: dark in colour, thick in texture, strong and acidic in taste.

On the way to the market we gave a lift to a very thin man wearing a dark suit. He stayed with us for a while as we did our shopping. At one point some money changed hands between him and one of our party. After he left us, they showed me the coins he gave as change: on one side they were covered with a sort of dark brown gum. Opium. In the time of the Shāh, pensioners who were addicted to opium could get their weekly dose with a kind of ration card that they showed in pharmacies to obtain little cylindrical bars the colour of milk coffee and as hard as caramel. Each bore an official paper seal, like a postage stamp. The pensioners used only part of their ration and made a little money on the side selling the rest; there was always some kid who got hold of his grandmother's opium. In those days the penalty for trafficking was death, and the State was attempting to dismantle the illegal drug market by supplying long-term addicts with high-quality opium, free of impurities. This kept a sector of the population calm and happy, no trouble to their families or to the country. With the Revolution, the death penalty for traffickers remained, but the supply to addicts was stopped. The new policy was to detoxify and rehabilitate the drug users; all those who wanted to take advantage of the new programme were asked to put their names down on the local register of people to be admitted to hospital for treatment. The Islamic government has put a lot of effort into this strategy, but the problem hasn't gone away, nor is it really being solved. Without films or music, the people of Tehrān don't have anything to do if they go out, so they get together at home and kill time smoking opium over a charcoal burner, passing around the tulip-shaped pipe, to which they hold a glowing coal with a pair of tongs. These days the opium is expensive and of poor quality.

Back at the house, we got straight into the caviar, which was the first course of a copious meal. Caviar on pieces of flat bread and vodka from the demijohn. In this house the men do the cooking.

Iranians are not particularly fond of caviar; in fact, most of them don't like it at all. As a visitor you soon realise that if someone offers you caviar, they're doing it to treat you, because they know that Westerners expect to eat caviar in Iran. But this prestigious and extremely expensive foodstuff is not part of the normal diet of Iranian families, nor is it used in the dishes prepared for special occasions. It is not even mentioned in books on traditional Iranian cooking.

Caviar is a source of income for Iran; tons of it are exported to the United States and Europe, and to Russia, where they change the labels and export it again. If I had to choose a colour to characterise Iran, I would choose black: the colour worn by the women and the men, the colour of the crêpe that decorates the streets and houses during religious celebrations, the colour of the country's riches – oil and caviar.

Iranian caviar should be eaten on a piece of toast or dry

bread, and it should be savoured in small quantities, spreading it over the tongue like a sort of butter with a slightly salty and extremely delicate flavour. Beluga caviar is the most highly reputed and expensive kind. It's dark grey and very fatty, almost like gelatine with little grey balls in it. When it's in your mouth you can't even feel the little balls, which sets it apart from the substitutes, especially the artificial ones, in which the balls sometimes feel like they're popping. Western restaurants usually serve it with onion, lemon and chopped hard-boiled egg, but with all those additives, even authentic sturgeon caviar can taste like it's made from salmon eggs or artificial substitutes.

Caviar is hard to digest. I remember the day I met some Spanish journalists in the foyer of the Intercontinental Hotel who had been given a kilo of caviar. They told me they could hardly wait to get into it with soup spoons, and so they did: they went up to their room with a couple of spoons borrowed from the kitchen and had their feast. The next day they were extremely ill.

Each time I went to Iran before the Revolution, I would always bring back a small round blue tin of caviar. They were sold officially in the airport, but everyone knew they were cheaper on the black market. The problem was that fresh caviar went off quickly, and when it did, it could be deadly. So you had to know who to buy it from. Somebody told me to go to a certain street in the south, where the dealers were, and to wait until I saw a man with one arm: he would be the one. Feeling sceptical and a bit scared, I went to the south, prompted by my taste for adventure but not at all sure I would find what I was looking for, so you can imagine my surprise when after wandering for just a few minutes in that bustling street, I saw the man with one arm. He was to become my regular supplier during those years. I never learnt his name.

In exotic places, you can imagine yourself starring in various films, and the film with the caviar, with the ice-cold vodka, the blue-eyed blond in the white linen suit and the restaurant full of mirrors, has always been a favourite of mine. Naturally, I'm wearing high heels and a fine silk dress. And if there is an orchestra or a pianist, and I can feel the warmth of his body close by, Tehrān is Casablanca.

The guys from the gambling den up in the attic break for a snack; then, gradually, they get back into the game. I wonder if I'll find out when they sleep.

Everyone is talking about their relatives in other countries – Europe, the United States, Australia – and many are trying to get visas themselves. It's a topic that keeps coming up.

In the afternoon we had tea in a hotel that used to be one of the most luxurious in Iran, the Hyatt Regency Caspian. It was swarming: the hallways, gardens and lounges were full of families who had come for a walk or for tea, like us. In the middle of all the shoving, a grim-faced woman in a *chādor* told us sharply to fix up our headscarves. This would turn out to be my only encounter with religious hate during the whole trip. The woman in question wasn't out for a walk, or going to have tea, or with her family, she was fulfilling a duty, and I don't know if she was a member of some organisation, or if she had taken it upon herself to play the role of moral guardian in that depraved place. Before the Revolution, very few Iranians would have crossed the threshold of this or any other luxury hotel belonging to one of the international chains. Now, anyone can take a walk in the gardens and relax in the lounge rooms.

Back at the house, a boy and a girl, brother and sister, fifteen and seventeen years old, spent the day moving from one armchair to another, listening to a Michael Jackson cassette. They only livened up at night, when someone put on some traditional music and they got up and danced in the Persian style, with suggestive contortions, arms held high, spinning, smiling and darting glances. Then, one by one, all the men began to dance, and the party got going to the rhythm of clapping hands. Meanwhile, up in the attic, the gambling continued.

The trip to the Caspian left me with a vaguely bitter taste in my mouth, and the impression of something falling apart, unhealthy, depressing and hopeless. The weather didn't help. So different from the way I would feel after the days we spent in Kāshān and Nā'īn, in the desert, among oases and simple, courteous people.

3 April

Chālūs – Caspian Sea

TODAY is the thirteenth day after New Year, and the last day of the holidays. In all the houses there are trays of sprouting seeds, like circular green brushes. The seeds were planted for Nō Rūz, and today people will place the trays on their cars so that when they drive off, the seeds will be scattered on the ground. They are called *sabzī*, which means green-coloured, and are one of the symbolic things beginning with 's' set out on a table specially prepared for New Year in each household: in the middle goes the *sabzī* and around it are placed apples (*sīb*), garlic (*sīr*), vinegar (*serké*), a gold coin (*sekeh*), a bowl with goldfish in it, a mirror, some coins in a dish, bread, trinkets and a copy of the Quran. The whole family gathers around the table at the moment when the year changes, and the sun moves into Aries. The mother is supposed to eat as many hard-boiled eggs as she has children, and even those mothers who never eat eggs do their best, to everyone's amusement. The eggs are placed in front of the mirror that adorns the Nō Rūz table. According to an old legend, the eggs move when the year changes, because the earth rests on the horn of a mythological bull (who lives in turn on the back of a huge whale in the sea) and after carrying it for a year on one horn, the bull gets tired and has to shift it across to the other.

Nō Rūz is celebrated with the family, in the privacy of homes closed to the outside world; the women wear bright colours, the children run around – children have a wonderful time in Iran: women make a great fuss of them and men treat them very gently – there is plenty of eating, talking, laughter, singing and dancing. In the end, everything in Iran revolves around the family, and it has always been that way. In hard times, the family helps you to survive; a cousin finds you a job, a brother-in-law sorts out your visa, or the brother of your uncle's wife who has always contributed generously to the mosque gets you out of jail.

In Tehrān, on the thirteenth day after Nō Rūz, you see lots of cars with *sabzī* on the roof, and the streets end up covered with crushed shoots. According to tradition, the *sabzī* should be scattered far from home in order to keep bad luck away. Now that people have cars, it is customary to put the sprouts on the roof or the bonnet so that they go flying off at high speed. Here in Chālūs, I have seen only two cars with sprouting lentils, and although there are some in the entrance of the house where I am staying, nobody has said anything about going to scatter them or about tying knots in the grass. Traditionally people go out into the country or to a park to tie knots in blades of grass. Each knot corresponds to a wish, and if the wind unties the knot, the wish will come true. Today I went into the garden to tie knots, as I did twenty years ago in Farah Park in Tehrān. That time, the wind untied nearly all my knots.

Iranians living in other countries must be celebrating Nō Rūz too, perhaps in a cold flat in Hamburg, or a house with a garden in a residential suburb of Chicago. Many are organising their return, and most hope to move back to Iran when they retire. They all dream of subtle pleasures hidden behind adobe walls and fragrant roses in the gardens of Iran, a country that displays only its sad and dark exterior.

Although it is customary to celebrate the thirteenth day with a meal in the country, or at least outside in a place where both rich and poor put blankets on the grass and enjoy a day in the open air, we were treated to a delicious feast at the house.

More relatives arrived, among them an old woman with a girl who must be about seventeen and has Down's syndrome. Their arrival caused great excitement; everyone went out into the garden to say hello and make a fuss of them. I had met the woman on a previous trip, and the girl too; she was little then, just able to walk. Seeing them, my mind went back to the unforgettable moments I spent with one of the old woman's daughters, the girl's mother, in the foyer of the Hilton, where I used to stay when I visited Tehrān, and where she worked as a prostitute. I had met her at her mother's house, and seen her just a couple of times. The day I ran into her at the entrance of the hotel, she greeted me warmly, and for a moment I was worried about getting a bad reputation. But then I realised I had one already, simply because I was a foreign woman travelling on my own; it was obvious from the way most of the men working in the luxury hotels, especially the younger ones, gave me a little smile. That was in the old days; now, with the *chādor*, no-one even remembers that foreign women exist. The temptation has disappeared, which was the idea after all.

From that day on, I would meet Nuri, as she was called (in Spain, our Nuris are named after the Virgin of Nuria, but in Iran the name means 'glowing with light'), between eleven and midnight in the foyer of the Hilton, and glass in hand, leaning against the grand piano, we would chat and listen to the melodies played especially for us by the Spanish pianist.

47

For her, it was a chance to take a break, while with the day's work behind me, I would let myself drift in the sweet nostalgia provoked by a mediocre *Guantanamera*. She told me about her adventures with oil millionaires, and was proud of the fact that from time to time she was called to the Shāh's Palace. Nuri had slightly damaged skin, but she was tall, slim and above all powerfully attractive; when she wore her red dress and high heels and came into the piano room with her black hair loose and her defiant coal-black gaze, all eyes turned to watch her. It was like a hurricane passing.

She spoke affectionately of her little girl, and said that with her work there were always deformities, it was an occupational hazard, but she gave me the impression that it wasn't a problem; the grandmother looked after the girl. In Iran's big families, everyone had a place, and naturally Bubu, as the girl was called, had hers too.

The grandmother remembered me and gave me an affectionate hug. (She is Mongolian and comes from the northern provinces where Chinggis Khaan left some of his hordes. Small and tough, she's brought up a mob of children and grandchildren on her own. In her house there has always been a place at the table for whoever's needed a meal. Including me. She and her granddaughter are short and stocky, with Asiatic features, but the difference between their faces is the difference between normality and subnormality.) Bubu was wearing a kilt and a red angora jumper with a round collar and short sleeves, a pearl necklace and a gold bracelet; she greeted everyone, distributing kisses, laughing at jokes, but went right past me, without a glance in my direction, as if I wasn't there.

I noticed that Irene was moved. I knew she had been looking forward to seeing them again, because the grandmother was the one who stood by her when, so many years ago now, she arrived from London, recently married, and was plunged into this immense and unfamiliar country, where she felt alone and lost. And it was Rave, the grandmother, who, some years later, helped her to bear the long ordeal of looking after a child with a serious illness, and then gradually to rebuild her life without the child. Rave made her hot soup, dressed and fed her other children, and put them to bed night after snowbound night through an interminable Tehrān winter, when Irene was on the point of breaking down.

Rave was one of the thirteen wives of Bahram's father, a general in the Shāh's army. He met her during one of his campaigns against the northern tribes. She was fourteen at the time, and she stole his heart. When the general moved on, falling in love and getting married again, it was Rave who looked after a good number of the children he had with his other twelve wives. Including Bahram, who was the son of one of the others. In short, she was the archetypal mother: there mightn't have been much money in her house, but everyone got by without a fuss. Rave kept chickens and had a vegetable garden, so there was always something to eat. It was so pleasant in Rave's house, so safe, so welcoming and warm, that even the general used to hole up there, when he was perilously wasted after a long string of alcoholic nights. She would make him hot broth and feed it to him in little spoonfuls, day after day, until his ravaged stomach could take it. She put cloths soaked in mysterious infusions on his forehead and washed his feet while giving him comforting massages. He would arrive at Rave's house a wreck, practically dead, and he always left every bit the general, with all his imposing presence restored, ready to break hearts and wreak havoc among the ranks. He

49

was very tall and slim; his eyes were blue and he had a big nose. Blue eyes are not common in Iran, and they usually belong to foreigners. Iranian eyes are dark and compact, all of a piece, coal-bright and piercing. Like planets in the night sky, they reflect light, but seem to shine with light of their own, as stars do. The general's eyes were transparent, clear and serene, and seemed to have concentrated all the skies of Asia. When he was weak, he could trust no-one but Rave, because during those spells anyone could have done him in with a simple shove, and he must have had many enemies. He was a powerful man, trusted by the Shāh, who had put him in charge of buying arms for the whole army. That's the sort of power he had. He was spectacularly stripped of his rank one day when, against the Shāh's orders, he bought a large consignment of tanks from the USSR instead of from the United States. He nearly lost his head as well as his rank that day, but the monarch had mercy, in consideration of the general's rock-solid loyalty, believing he had done it for the good of Iran, even though he knew it might cost him his life. The general always gave alms to beggars in the street – sometimes he would just put his hand in his pocket and give away all the money he had on him. He was prone to falling madly in love, and made a great fuss of the current woman, showering her with gifts. He got married with a certain regularity, and naturally kept having children; the previous wife was more or less forgotten and left in a precarious economic situation. And so it went on: Rave would come along and pick up the pieces, thinking nothing of it. She had the impossible task of looking after that herd of children: they always had enough to eat, but it was harder to make sure that they all had shoes. Bahram remembers leaving home each morning carrying his shoes, and walking all the way to school barefoot (and it was a long way) so as not to wear them out. Before climbing the last hill, he would sit down on a big stone, always the same one, and put them on.

In several of the houses we've visited over the past few days I have seen framed photos of the general; in each case it turned out to be the house of one of his ex-wives, and all of them kept him prominently on display in the dining room, wearing his peaked cap, with its gilt embroidered crest depicting a lion armed with a sword facing a rising sun, the symbol of Imperial Iran.

I asked about Nuri, and was told she was in Hamburg. She went because of the Revolution, like many doctors, lawyers, lecturers and architects. Prostitutes emigrated too. She left Bubu with Rave.

The meal was a feast of white fish from the Caspian and various kinds of rice, with saffron, sweet oranges, *serej* (a kind of small, acidic red raisin), flat bread, soft white cheese, *sabzī* and yoghurt. What I really like is the *tadīg*, a kind of burnt crust from the bottom of the pan the rice was cooked in, which is served on a separate dish. *Tadīg* is crunchy and delicious, and has its enthusiasts in every household; it's a bit like the burnt bottom of a Valencia paella, but while it's considered bad form to have burnt bits in a paella, Iranian rice is not what it should be unless it has a good *tadīg*. Iranians are always amused to learn that I am among the crust fans, and we joke and laugh about it.

A man with a mischievous face asked me: "Do you know what the difference is between Iran under the Shāh and Iran under Khomeinī? Before, Iranians went out to drink and came home to pray, now it's the other way round, they come home to drink and go out to pray."

Apparently, getting back to Tehrān is going to be terrible. Traffic jams. We decide to take it easy and leave tomorrow morning. The holidays are over, and in the house the packing up has started.

4 April

The orchids of the Caspian

*H*AVING returned to Tehrān, we decide to visit our friends the Goldars, who have hothouses for growing orchids near Nōshar, back on the Caspian coast. They're not at home, but their overseer welcomes us. We recognise one another; he was already working here twenty years ago, and since he looks just as young as he did then, I suppose he must have been a boy at the time, though he seemed grown up to me. He tells us that during Khomeinī's Revolution, they confiscated the hothouses and handed them over to the local Revolutionary council. During that period up to two hundred people worked here. Now the business is back in the hands of its old owner, who moved to London after the troubles, but has returned to look after his flowers again. He has reorganised the staff, and now there are thirty workers on the plantation, the same ones as before the Revolution. A high-tech automatic system heats the thirty sheds with warm, humid air. All the flowers are sold in Tehrān, with consignments leaving every day.

During the Nō Rūz holidays of 1974, when I was spending a few days with the Goldars and their four little daughters at the house in Nōshar, the then prime minister, Amir Abbas Hoveīda, came to visit. He was an orchid enthusiast and grew them with his wife, who had a degree in biology from the

Sorbonne. Wearing an orchid in the buttonhole of his jacket, as was his habit, Hoveīda looked over the hothouses and remarked that perhaps he would bring his own orchids there one day for safekeeping. When Khomeinī took over, Hoveīda was imprisoned, judged and executed. The overseer took us to the hothouse where Hoveīda's orchids are still kept, and tended with care. A few days later, in Tehrān, we would be shown a video of Hoveīda's confession, broadcast on television just before the execution. In the video he wasn't wearing an elegant suit with an orchid, but what looked like a pair of striped pyjamas. The first thing he did was to apologise to the Iranian people for appearing before them in such a state, then, with dignity, he asked to be forgiven if he had caused them any harm during his term as prime minister, and he finished by listing the prices of various items, such as a pencil, a textbook and an exercise book, and he asked all Iranians to remember what he was saying. I was told that at the time, people thought he must have been so perturbed by his situation that he had become incoherent. Today, the prices of these items are exorbitant. It gave me goosebumps. I remember him as he was that day in the hothouses at Nōshar: he seemed an elegant man, though physically he was in fact rather short and fat, a bit like Carlo Ponti; he spoke good French, was very cultivated, and did not have children. At the time I thought this a sign of modernity and independence, in a country where men insist on having children no matter what, and repudiate infertile wives. For the people of Iran, in the heart of the country, with its narrow bazaars and weightlifters' gymnasiums, Hoveīda was one of the figureheads of a corrupt state, channelling oil money into private accounts. The Shāh and Hoveīda had a single objective: economic development, and they believed that this was the way to solve all of Iran's problems. For them, democracy and the cultural identity of the country were secondary. In his book on Islam, *Among the Believers*, V. S. Naipaul recounts that four months after the execution, in Ghom, he met the Ayatollāh Khalkhalī, the Revolutionary judge who had condemned thousands of Iranians to death. For him, the execution of Hoveīda was like a trophy. Shortly after the event, in an interview published in the *Tehrān Times*, he calmly described how the first bullet hit the condemned man in the neck, without killing him, so the executioner ordered him to hold his head up, and as soon as he did so, a second bullet hit him in the brow. Khalkhalī affirmed that he had kept the gun used to carry out the deed. When asked if he had fired the shots himself, he said no, the gun had been given to him by a Revolutionary guard, no doubt the one who had pulled the trigger.

5 April

Tehrān

I DON'T know if it was the caviar, the home-made vodka or the water up north, but the fact is I've got a case of the runs that's going to give me plenty of opportunities to check out the state of the country's toilets over the next few days. Report to follow.

Down on Ferdōsī Avenue, the dollar is now worth 2460 *rials.* I changed a hundred-dollar bill, and was given four bundles that won't fit into my pocket.

In the afternoon we go to Rave's house for tea; she greets us with open arms, and serves the tea with little pistachio cakes, flat like tarts, round and green. They're delicious. Irene has brought a present for Bubu from Barcelona: a beauty kit full of cosmetics, creams, powders, red lipsticks, pearl-coloured nail-polish and glass-bead necklaces. Bubu is thrilled, but her cousins start teasing her and she gets cross and goes red; something they said about a boy has embarrassed her and made her blush. Although she is basically good-natured, she goes sulky, then gets fed up and with a very serious air says four words I can't catch. When people are gently making fun of her, she can stop them in their tracks. I realise that she is, in fact, very proud.

In the kitchen, the meal is being prepared; we're staying for dinner. Rave is coming and going, listening without speaking, but the look on her face betrays a certain worry, borne with Eastern patience and resignation. She gives me the family photo albums and finds me a place on the sofa at the edge of the conversation. Bubu is sitting in front of me, in an armchair, painting her nails rose-pearl: quiet, busy and pensive, from time to time she says a few words I can't understand and laughs to herself. The family is talking about her, what she might do in the future, and about far-off countries. I watch her and wonder what she is feeling: anxiety, probably, but I don't know how to communicate with her, and she hasn't even looked at me since we arrived. For her, I don't even exist. The only thing I can do is smile at her when she looks up, but I can tell she's looking straight through me as if were transparent. There's no sign of recognition.

A bit later on, while I'm busy looking at the photos of Nuri in Hamburg, I feel somebody sit down very close beside me. It's Bubu, come to look at the photos with me. I don't move, or say anything, or even look at her, so as not to break the spell. I let the warmth of our bodies touching take care of the communication. After a few long, precarious minutes, Bubu starts showing me the photos, pointing out Nuri each time she appears and laughing happily. In spite of my shaky Fārsī and her opaque speech, we understand each other perfectly. In these moments shared with Bubu, life is sweet.

The group around the table on the other side of the room is in a constant state of flux. Relatives keep arriving and sitting down, while the others squash up to make room. They are talking about Nuri, Bubu, visas, Hamburg, Australia and Sweden. I can tell it's an important conversation, and that the family is planning its future in a faraway country.

The news is that Rave's children and grandchildren, the ones left in Iran with whom she and Bubu live, have just obtained visas to emigrate to Australia, and must leave within two months. In this short space of time they have to organise their departure and sell their apartment, because they need the money for the trip. The problem is working out what will happen to Rave and Bubu. Rave is old, her sight is very weak, and she needs medical attention. She suffers from intense pain (she points to her cheek as she explains) caused by a herpes zoster infection, and she uses opium to make it bearable. Apparently there is a very good specialist in Barcelona . . . Ideally, she would end up living in Hamburg with Nuri, or in Sweden with the family of one of her other children. But even if Rave could get a visa, Bubu wouldn't have a chance, they say. No developed country is going to take in a mongoloid girl, especially not from Iran. What a world, I think, as I sit listening to the conversation and feeling clammy. The warmth of Bubu's body close beside me gives me comfort. My heart is telling me that Bubu shouldn't leave Iran: she's at ease here, knows the language and manages well in this environment; she's safe and happy. I don't know why this problem, which is really none of my business, has begun to bother me.

The couple who have managed to obtain visas are happy, and can't pass up the opportunity to leave the country and start a new life. They have two children – a boy of fifteen and a girl of seventeen – who are stifled by the contradictions of life in Tehrān. They want them to go to a good school and get a good education, rather than spending all day in front of the television zapping from channel to foreign channel and dreaming of another world. All their close relatives have already left and now their big chance has come. It has taken them years, and cost them all their savings: many *tōmāns* have had to change hands discreetly to clear all sorts of bureaucratic obstacles from their path. And now, at last, the moment has come to make the break. They chose Australia because they have friends there who emigrated a few years ago and already have a shop. Their friends have told them that they could set up a shop too and that the Australian government will help them, especially with the children.

Hand in hand on the sofa, Bubu and I eat a delicious stew with lentils and dried lemon, while watching the video of Nō Rūz in Hamburg last year, with Nuri surrounded by Iranians of all ages, proposing toasts, eating, dancing, laughing and kidding around, like people anywhere in the world when they celebrate with family and friends.

While we're eating, a racket drowns out the conversation. The kids have put a Michael Jackson video on, and there he is on the screen, contorting himself and yelling, at full volume.

On the way home in the car, Irene and Bahram talk about the problem with Rave and the girl. Almost everyone is saying they can't stay in Tehrān, because they won't have an apartment, and since none of Rave's children will be left in the country, some other relative would have to take them in and look after them. Although Bahram is not convinced, Irene thinks that the first thing to do is to get Rave to see Dr Barraquer in Barcelona before she goes blind. She's determined to help, and prepared to do whatever it takes to make this consultation happen. And where Rave goes, Bubu has to go as well. Irene can be like a steamroller; when she gets a project into her head, she'll move heaven and earth to carry it out. I am beginning to realise that the aim of her current crusade is to take Rave and Bubu to Barcelona, and see about the rest later . . .

Before bed, Bahram and his mother recite poetry for us, hand in hand. Quite amazing. Some relatives and neighbours drop by, as they do each day, and join in the recital. All Iranians know lots of poems, by Hāfez, Sa'dī, Ferdōsī . . . and they like to recite them when they get together. One starts off, then another takes over, and it's a moving experience for everybody. Bahram's mother brings over the thick volume of Hāfcz's poems and gives it to me to open at any page. The poem will reveal my destiny. They read it aloud. The poem says I will share the aroma of wine and the scent of Golestāni roses with the poor and the footloose, and that my heart's thirst for foreign lands will never be quenched. For me it's a moment of glory. Then the book changes hands, and the ceremony continues. Wherever in the world two Iranians meet, chances are they will end up hand in hand reciting poetry. Bricklayers at work don't sing, they recite poems by Omar Khayyām. In Iran, poetry has always been the way to resist oppression; its coded language fosters wordplay, and helps lovers, members of the underground and everyone, in the end, to sublimate aspirations that can't be realised in this wretched world.

6 April

Towards Kāshān

$\mathcal{W}$E leave Tehrān at dawn, heading south this time. We drive by the bazaar, pass the big cemetery on our right and, once we are out of the city, see the tongues of flame rising from the oil refinery.

I have been in the Tehrān cemetery once; it was when I was a student, following the death of a classmate's mother. This classmate was the leader of the group of Kurdish students at the University of Tehrān, of whom I will have more to say later. That day, posters appeared on the doors of all the faculties announcing the sad event and explaining that buses would be leaving from each faculty in the afternoon to transport those students who wished to attend the funeral. The news spread through the university and the residential college where I was living. As a friend of the girlfriend of the son of the deceased, I was supposed to attend the burial. All the girls attending had to wear a black *chādor*, though I don't know where they got them from since most of them never wore one, and I doubt that they even had one packed away. I was lent a *chādor*, and it was then that I realised for the first time how hard they are to wear if you are not used to it.

It was a beautiful sunny spring afternoon. We got into the buses that were waiting for us at the gates of the faculty decorated with large wreaths of white flowers. Inside the bus I was travelling in there was a fridge full of Coca-Cola and other cool drinks, which we handed around and cheerfully consumed during the trip. We were met at the cemetery by our classmate, the son of the deceased, elegantly dressed in a dark suit, standing in front of an impressive esplanade made up of white paving stones alternating with square beds of roses in bloom, in a chequerboard pattern. The women separated from the men and moved into a rectangular room with chairs all along the walls, on which female relatives were already sitting. More women kept arriving, all wearing black *chādor*s, until there were no seats left. In front of the chairs were long, low tables, on which boxes of tissues had been strategically placed. The doors were shut, and the voice of the mullah began to filter through the loudspeakers set up in the room. The voice grew clearer and more intense, until it levelled off in a kind of chanting. I couldn't understand what the mullah was saying, but I guessed he was speaking of the deceased, because periodically all the mourners were seized by an intense emotion and began to weep and sigh. A multitude of hands reached simultaneously for the boxes on the tables. Meanwhile, tea was served. Seated in front of me was a beautiful, elegant woman wearing a semi-transparent *chādor* that was like a large shawl, under which you could just make out a close-fitting black dress. A bracelet of thick gold chain shone on each wrist. The elegy went on for almost two hours. At first the atmosphere seemed oppressive, but after a while, and no doubt because of the incantation completely filling the room, I entered an almost beatific state, in which time didn't count. When we left the room, the long shadows of the rose bushes were stencilled on the paving stones.

We've just overtaken a truck with a Trabosa trailer. Throughout the trip to the south we keep seeing these Trabosas. In 1975, the Spanish company that makes them, in Mollet del Vallés, went up against the major players and won a contract to provide more than two thousand trailers to Iran, and for a couple of years I helped Mr Bartomeu, the president of the company, to carry out the operation. The trailers were towed away from Mollet by Mercedes trucks driven by Korean drivers, flown in specially from Korea on chartered planes. A lot of these trailers were hauled around Iran and, as I have seen, some are still on the road, but many others were abandoned in the desert, quickly forgotten and soon useless, after sand got into their moving parts. This waste was a result of the way Iranian commissions were collected in Switzerland: the bigger the order, the bigger the commission, and it was with this sort of buying policy that the country worked out what it did and didn't need. If a contract signed with a humble company from Mollet del Vallés blew out like this, you can imagine what must have been going on with the huge contracts signed every day in the Shāh's prodigal Iran. It was as if they were setting things up for the sword of Islam to come and make a clean sweep, putting an end to the excesses.

We pull up at a tollgate decorated with photos of the Emām Khomeinī and the *ayatollāhs* Rafsanjānī, Khalkhalī, Khameneī . . . I count forty-five of them, all bearded and wearing black or white turbans, depending on whether or not they are direct descendants of the prophet. Khomeinī, of course, has a black one. He is a *seyed*, which means a descendant of Mohammed; for this reason, and because he is the 'guide' of the community, the Iranian Revolutionaries gave him the title of Emām when he came back to Iran in 1979, after fifteen years of exile. On the left, we see the new mosque where he is buried, with its dome and four minarets. Beside the mosque, a large building is going up to house the Islamic University.

Since we left Tehrān, the road has been bordered by rows of recently planted pine trees. They are just over a metre tall, and we will see them for many kilometres. Apparently they want to plant them all the way to Ghom. There must be thousands of them, green and healthy; I ask how they are watered, but no-one knows. Beyond the pines the landscape is harsh and arid, with white patches of salt, like the Badlands of South Dakota, the backdrop for many a Western. The Salt Lake stretches away on our left. Distant mountains are reflected in the water and a broad border of brilliant white surrounds the lake, like a cloth under a cake, a cloth of salt. Green plains covered with low bushes stretch off to ranges of low, rounded mountains on the horizon. The lake is blurred by different shades of mist, from grey to white. As we travel south, the landscape changes to brown and green; from time to time we see a village made up of adobe cubicles stuck together, with skylights in the middle of their rounded roofs. In the heart of the desert, we pass through an agricultural zone which is astoundingly green and luxuriant.

On the outskirts of Ghom, the holy city, a football field appears out of the desert, with two goals made of sticks and players in yellow. Today is a holiday, a religious feast, and black flags are hanging from all the lamp posts. It's a sad day, commemorating the martyrdom of the third Shi'ite Emām.

Seen from the highway, Ghom is a big city, with two-storey houses, all the colour of adobe, blue domes and shining minarets reaching up to pierce the sky. The domes of the Great Mosque rise above the others, one blue, the other gold, surrounded by high minarets. I counted six. Back in the nine-teenth century, Fath Alī Shāh had the city restored at great cost and the dome of the old mosque covered with gold mosaics. He is buried beside it along with other shāhs descended from Abbās I. The mosque houses the tomb of Bibi Fātemé, the sis-ter of the Eighth Emām, Emām Rezā, in a marble and gold mausoleum surrounded by a grille of solid silver. It is one of the most important destinations for pilgrims in Iran.

Ghom is also an important centre for Islamic studies and publishing, attracting students from all over the Shi'ite world. There are fourteen thousand students, each wearing their mul-lah's garb: a pastel-coloured cotton shirt with buttons up to the neck and a long black or dark brown coat. On their heads they wear a black or white turban. V. S. Naipaul compares Ghom to Oxford in the Middle Ages, but in Ghom there are no imposing university buildings – there isn't even a university. The teachers aren't employed by anyone. It's up to the stu-dents to choose the scholar with whom they want to study. If he accepts them, the students go to the place where he lives and dispenses his learning, in one of the city's many *madrasés*, or schools of Islamic studies. If a teacher is mediocre, he won't get students; if the standard of his teaching lapses, his students will leave him. An Islamic master is recognised as such for his ability to win over an audience. It's the students who make the teacher and give him approval. More than a simple teacher, the master should be a guide, a model, an example to imitate in every aspect of life.

The study of Islam can last a lifetime. Some students stay for six years, others for twelve, twenty, even thirty. The many subjects they study include Arabic, grammar, logic, rhetoric, literature, Islamic philosophy, law and jurisprudence. There is no predetermined syllabus, nor are there any exams. Each student needs a different amount of time to become an expert in the interpretation of the holy books, and together the teacher and student work out how long it will take. As the years go by, the student has opportunities to see whether or not he is capable of holding his own in a high-level theological discussion, conducted in the esoteric language he has been struggling to learn, not just with his master and guide, but also with other eminent theologians. It will be obvious to him when he has gone as far as he can. If he comes up against a barrier his intellect will never penetrate, however many years he spends trying, it's time to quit. For the duration of his studies, the student lives at the expense of the theologian, who gives him shelter, food and even sometimes a small allowance. With time, he will become a mullah, and if he is a brilliant student, an *ayatollāh*. The young men who choose to go to *madrasés* know that they are choosing a life of austerity, without material rewards, although they do acquire great prestige. In the last hundred years, all the great theologians have studied at Ghom, or at the other great centre of Shi'ite learning, Najaf in Iraq, where Ali, the son-in-law of the Prophet, is buried. It was here in Ghom that Khomeinī dispensed his teachings before he was expelled from the country by the Shāh, and it was here that he came to live when he returned to Iran.

Financially, the Islamic schools are completely independent of the state. That is their strength. A study carried out by the Tehrān Institute for Social Research in 1966 showed that 85 per cent of the students in these schools were from farming families, 10 per cent came from the bazaars and 5 per cent from clerical families. Even today, the *madrasés* provide a real chance for boys from the country with a calling and the right disposition. Leaving aside the obvious differences, seminaries used to perform much the same function in Castile and other parts of Spain until not so long ago: farming families, struggling to support all their children, could give their boys an education by sending them to the seminary. And if they ended up becoming priests, all the better.

Most of the men governing Iran today are the sons of farmers who went through the Islamic schools. In the time of the Shāh, the technocrats and political leaders had received secular educations in Iranian private schools or abroad, and came from urban upper or middle-class backgrounds. Since the state schools and the secular private schools were not sufficient for the whole population of the country, especially in rural areas, the Islamic schools sprang up, preparing a different class of leaders, ignored by the State until the Revolution mobilised them. Today's leaders acquired a solid education in the religious schools, but the authoritarian nature of the old regime excluded them from the centres of power for decades. The Shāh thought he could do without them when the country's economy was booming thanks to Western technology and petrodollars. And he based the justice system on laws written to reflect Western legal practice, which defended only the rich and the strong.

Things came to a head in 1963, when Khomeinī was expelled from Ghom and took up residence in Najaf. That was when the movements which had sprung up around the schools and the mosques joined forces to constitute a real resistance, a development assisted by the total absence of unions and community groups, a consequence of the prohibition of political parties. Social and community activities were only tolerated in a religious context.

When thinking about the importance of teaching in the

gradual gestation of Iran's Islamic Revolution, it is worth remembering that the Quran was revealed to Mohammed during a twenty-year period of preaching (612–632), first in Mecca, then in Medina. It was written down a few years after the death of the Prophet. The first commentator or interpreter of the Quran was Mohammed himself, and he was followed by disciples and friends who wrote commentaries on his commentaries. The Quran and the Prophet's commentaries (the Hadith) form the basis for Muslim ethics and law, and consequently, for education in Islamic countries.

During my years as a student at the University of Tehrān, I visited Ghom on one occasion with the cultural attaché from the Spanish embassy, along with his wife and the chargé d'affaires. At that time, foreigners were absolutely forbidden to enter the area surrounding the tomb of Bibi Fātemé, the major pilgrimage destination in Ghom. Since I spoke some Persian, we asked for an audience with the *ayatollāh* in charge of the area, hoping we would be granted permission to visit the tomb. Along with the other women in the party, I had duly equipped myself with a *chādor* hired from a stand. Now there is no need to hire *chādor*s, because women no longer leave the house uncovered, as they did in the time of the Shāh, so all that commercial activity around the mosques has disappeared. Our presence was announced to the *ayatollāh*, who came out to meet us straight away at the gate of the mosque. I politely explained that we had come from Spain, where Muslims had lived for eight hundred years and had left marvellous mosques; that we felt Islam was part of our heritage, and had travelled to Ghom with the intention of visiting the tomb of Bibi Fātemé. Naturally, the *ayatollāh* already knew everything I said in my preamble, and I don't know if it was the Persian, the *chādor*s or the conviction with which we presented ourselves as pilgrims, but in any case, he let us go in on two conditions: that we didn't open our mouths, so no-one would know we were foreigners, and that we avoided any disturbances that might put us in physical danger. My acquaintances from the embassy, who had been in Iran for years, had never been to Ghom, and it had never occurred to them that they might be allowed into the sacred precinct. In order to enter it we had to take off our shoes, and it turned out that the chargé d'affaires had holes in his socks, with his big toes sticking through them. I had to stifle my laughter so as not to give myself away, but I'm sure that the holes in the socks of the man who is now a Spanish ambassador gave our group a more authentic look.

Ghom is surrounded by green, well-cultivated fields filled with little flocks of fat-bottomed sheep. In Iran, the sheep have pouches full of fat on their rumps. As we head further south, the highway leading to Kāshān is lined with curious buildings shaped like truncated cones, about as big as small houses, made of bricks, carefully laid in circular courses, with a hole at the bottom to let in air for combustion. Some of them have smoke coming out of the top. They are brick kilns. A great many bricks are made in Ghom, and their characteristic white or light yellow colour is particularly prized. Bahram says that when he was little, he and his sister used to play at making bricks, drying them in matchboxes, then using them to build little houses and gardens.

On our right there are low mountains like crouching iguanas with ridges along their backs; vivid spring has come to the intensely green plain, with fields of crops and trees emerging from their lethargy. Beside the highway there are gardens bordered with fig trees or surrounded by adobe walls and full of pomegranates and other flowering fruit trees. I catch a glimpse of the railway that runs from Ghom to Kermān.

We have just overtaken a scooter carrying a father, a mother wearing a *chādor*, a boy between the father's legs, and a girl between the father and the mother, also wearing a *chādor*. They seem quite comfortable, or at least accustomed to travelling in this way. During our trip we have seen many families getting around like this on motorbikes; helmets still aren't considered necessary, and I think about the extra difficulties it will create for women when they are.

The freeway with tollgates stops in Ghom; from there on, it's a single-lane highway.

The outskirts of Kāshān are like Eden, with their adobe-walled gardens full of fruit trees and poplars. But then the garages start to appear beside the highway, along with run-down warehouses, bits of twisted, rusting iron and houses in ruins. Before entering the city we pass a mosque made of bare bricks the colour of the desert; its cone-shaped cupola, decorated with glazed tiles, shines in the midst of decay.

We head straight for a *chelō kabāb*, a typical Iranian restaurant, where there is a single fixed menu consisting of white rice with pieces of roasted lamb, salad and yoghurt. Extracting ourselves from the car is a farce: the *chādor*s we have been wearing throughout the trip are all over the place, leaving the most compromising parts – hair and legs – uncovered. We have to rearrange ourselves in the middle of the street. I forgot to say that Bahram's mother lent each of us a *chādor* (the early start is catching up with me). Mine is black with little white flowers, and is made of fine, light cotton. The Islamic uniform of headscarf and overgarment is common in Tehrān but you don't see it much in the rest of the country; provincial women have always worn the *chādor*, and I think it's best to do likewise, as they will certainly appreciate the gesture. The *chādor* is a piece of cloth the size of a sheet; it has a straight edge, the middle of which is placed on the head, and the opposite edge, which is slightly rounded, reaches almost to the ground. There is only one seam: the one joining this rounded part to the bottom edge of the rectangle. Many women wear their *chādor*s on top of the *rūsārī*, because that way it slips less; and, naturally, this is what we are doing. The elegance with which Iranian women put on and wear the *chādor* is remarkable: they pop it over their head and hold one side between their teeth while preparing and gathering in the other side, or they hold the whole thing up under their chin with one hand, leaving the other hand free. But if they need to use both hands, they hold both sides of the *chādor* with their teeth. It isn't easy to wear a *chādor* if you're not used to it. An inexperienced woman runs the risk of having all her careful tucking come undone at any moment, and since it would be unthinkable to expose oneself in the street, Bahram's mother gave me a little clip shaped like a frog to hold the cloth under my chin and stop it from slipping. At first I tried it with the frog on the outside, but it was green and looked awful; then I worked out how to put it inside, which was a better solution anyway because my hands were inside too. By the end of the trip I had dispensed with the little frog; I no longer needed it. The *chādor* stayed up as if by magic, and I even started to like it. It was a pretext for laughter and kindness; it opened many doors and initiated conversations; it even allowed us to make friends.

Since today is a feast day, almost all the *chādor*s are black, and the women have put on their best, made of thick and fine satin, the dull and shiny surfaces composing patterns. At first all women in *chādor*s look the same, like pedestrian phantoms or upright beetles, but after a while it becomes possible to tell if the woman is young or old, fat or thin, and to recognise more subtle details, even from behind, judging from a gait, the grace with which the *chādor* is worn, a foot, a hand, a pair of eyes . . . it's quite an exercise in observation. "Sometimes, thanks to a gust of wind, it is as if the sum of Persian beauty were revealed in the blink of an eye," says Pierre Loti.

Religious music plays on the radio as we eat our meal in the restaurant. Every station in the country is playing this sort of music today, in memory of the third Emām Hussein and his followers, martyred at Karbala during the month of Moharram in the year 680. This is why the streets are decorated with black crêpe bearing inscriptions from the Quran, and the women are giving their very blackest *chādor*s an airing. It looks like Irene and I are the only ones wearing discreet little flowers. I guess we don't count though, because we are travellers. In Muslim countries, travellers have a special status. According to the Quran, one should help the traveller, who, like the sick person, is granted special permission to eat during the daylight hours of Ramadan. All other Muslims must fast. Bahram tells us that most Iranian Muslims are duodecimal Shi'ites, who recognise only twelve Emāms as descendants of Mohammed in the line of Ali, the Prophet's cousin and son-in-law. The twelfth Emām disappeared in 940, and he is the hidden, absent, hoped-for one, the one who is to come; and when he comes, the true Islamic State will be established, in which all men will be brothers, putting an end to fourteen centuries of exile and mourning in a hostile world.

According to the Prophet himself, the twelve Emāms are the community's only infallible guides, holding the keys to the meanings hidden in the versicles of the Quran. For Shi'ites, truth resides not in the spoken but in the hidden word. The search for the Quran's hidden meaning has given rise to a discipline based on the esoteric interpretation of the texts. The language of this discipline and the knowledge it unlocks are not accessible to everyone, only to those who have proved their worthiness through long study. That is why, as I said before, students spend so many years in the schools of Ghom, only some of them reaching the level of wisdom required to pursue the search to its furthest reaches. When the twelfth Emām comes again, there will be an end to the search for the hidden meaning of the prophecies (*valayat*).

When Islam arrived in Persia, the country already had a rich cultural history. It had known two thousand years of Elamite civilisation (2500–640 BC), the empire of the Medes and the Achaemenians (from the seventh to the fourth century BC), Alexander the Great's conquest and domination by the Macedonian dynasty of the Seleucids (fourth and third centuries BC), the nationalist reaction of the Parthians (from the third century BC to the second century AD) and the empire of the Sassanians, the most glorious period of the country's history.

With the expansion of Islam, struggles emerged between different religious groups for control of the empire. Then the Shi'ite movement appeared (656–661). The Shi'ites – the term comes from the expression *shi'at'Ali*, which means, literally, 'the party of Ali' – were the supporters of the Prophet's direct descendants, the family of Ali, who was the husband of Mohammed's daughter Fatima, and they were opposed to the

75

sovereignty of the Umayyads, whom they considered usurpers. Between 661 and 675, the Umayyad dynasty began the process of spreading Arab culture, and undertook an implacable military colonisation of the country. In 661 Ali was assassinated in Kufa (today called Najaf, in Iraq), and twenty years later the Prophet's grandson Hussein died in the massacre at Karbala, also in Iraq. Hussein was killed by the son of the Umayyad Caliph of Damascus, and his martyrdom has had great symbolic value for the Shi'ites ever since, as an ongoing reminder of the struggle against usurpers and oppressors.

The next caliphate was that of the Abbasids (750–1258), the dynasty descended from one of the Prophet's uncles. They moved the capital to Baghdad and practised political liberalism and tolerance in religious matters, which won them the support of the Persians, whose educated élites began to infiltrate the administration of the Islamic Empire. From the tenth century on, three hundred years after the birth of Islam, Persians participated actively in Islamic culture, and the country produced a stream of great philosophers, theologians, writers and scientists.

The Mongol hordes of Chinggis Khaan put an end to the Abbasids in 1258, with the conquest of Baghdad and the assassination of the last caliph. They had already pillaged the whole of Iran. It took centuries for the cultures of Islam and Iran to recover, but eventually the Mongols became Iranian and Muslim. They also became sedentary, which favoured the revival of cultural life. Under Mongol rule, Arabic lost its role as the language that held the culture of the country together, and Fārsī became dominant.

Just as Iran was beginning to recover from the Mongol invasion, the country was invaded and ravaged once again, this time by the Tartar Tamerlane, who overran the country in around 1380. His descendants (the Timurid dynasty) established cultivated and refined courts, in which literature and the sciences flourished once more.

The Timurids were succeeded by the Safavid dynasty, who secured the political unity of Iran, based on duodecimal Shi'ism. For the first time, the Shi'ites enjoyed political and religious freedom. They founded prestigious schools of theology and jurisprudence, and regained control of those that had managed to survive since the eleventh century, such as the schools of Najaf and Ghom. Although it was during the brilliant reign of Shāh Abbās I (1588–1629) that Esfahān became the monumental city it is today, and in spite of the progress made in the arts (especially in architecture), science and philosophy suffered setbacks under the Safavids, due to the formidable power acquired by the Shi'ite dignitaries and the schools they administrated. This power has been preserved up to the present day.

We install ourselves in Kāshān's best hotel, the Amīr Kabīr, a Hilton-type establishment built before the Revolution and confiscated by the Islamic committees. Now it is run by two rather shabby-looking brothers. The prices for foreigners are given in dollars, and are five times higher than those for Iranians. The *chādor*s make no difference here: it's the passports that count. The hotel is well on the way to decrepitude, an exhibition of rising damp, peeling paint and shoddy repairs. The bath is rusty; the hand basin and mirror are dirty. There is no toilet paper: the hotel doesn't supply it. To tell the truth, toilet paper is hard to find anywhere. During the time of the Shāh, a big effort was made to project an image of Iran as being up there with the most advanced countries, but now it has gone back to third-world ways. We haven't seen a single tourist staying in the hotel, or indeed anywhere in the city.

From the sixth floor there is a marvellous view over Kāshān and the surrounding countryside. A boy who works in the hotel restaurant offers to show us around in the afternoon. He takes us to his home in a suburb on the outskirts of town, filled with adobe houses the colour of desert sand or dust. At the end of a narrow, twisting alley, a door opens onto a patio where there is a puny tree and a tap. Up some stairs there is a long narrow room in which three girls are knotting an enormous carpet on a vertical loom. The carpet – twelve square metres of it – will be finished soon, but it has taken them two years, they say, because they haven't been able to spend many hours on it each day.

They are a family of Iraqi Kurds, who immigrated during the time of the Shāh. The father works at the hotel too; the mother is out at the moment, having a reading lesson. The grandmother is busy with pots and pans at the tap on the patio, and when Karim, our guide, introduces us as foreigners, she replies: "Are they? Like us!"

The three girls and the grandmother are wearing brightly coloured dresses, and their headscarves don't cover their long hair and beads. Two of the girls, aged fourteen and sixteen, are Karim's sisters, while the other one, who looks just as young, is his wife, and is pregnant. He tells us he is nineteen, and his wife seventeen. He says that all Kurds think about going home. For the millions of Iraqi Kurds in Iran, going back is virtually an obligation, simply because they are so numerous that the country is having trouble absorbing them. I ask him what language they speak, and he tells me that at home they continue to speak Kurdish.

I have fond memories of the Kurdish students I knew at the University of Tehrān. They came from Iraq too, and were doing doctorates in Persian Language and Literature. One was the grandson of General Barzani, the hero of the Kurdish resistance. During the vacations, they would go to fight in the mountains, and one came back after the Nō Rūz holiday mourning his brother who had been killed in a skirmish. They were very well mannered and serious, interested in everything that was happening in the world, and seemed to carry a great weight of responsibility on their shoulders. When they came back after the holidays they gave the girls in the class fluorescent pink nylon scarves decorated with droplets of transparent plastic, surrounded by little white embroidered birds. I still have the scarf they gave me, and I wear it from time to time, because I think it's pretty and because it reminds me of people who were good friends. Each time the topic of languages and dialects came up in class, Arabic and Persian with their various dialects being presented as the major languages which had served as vehicles for great civilisations, I would think "Here come the Kurds." And sure enough, one would raise their hand and launch into the usual speech, to the effect that Kurdish is not a dialect but a language, with its own literature, and that it is spoken by I don't know how many millions of people. As a Catalan, I identified with them. Divided among four nations, they have been struggling for centuries to obtain an independent Kurdish state, and have nearly attained their objective on a number of occasions, most recently during the Gulf War, but each time they have come off badly. Although Iraq gave them the right to autonomy in 1970, constant tension and skirmishes led to all-out war in 1974. In 1975 the rebellion was quelled in the wake of an agreement between Iran and Iraq regarding the River Shatt al-Arab and the cessation of Iranian aid.

My Kurdish friends invited me to come back and spend some time with them at the end of the academic year, but I didn't accept, because at the time I was fascinated by another country, on the other side of Iran, a country I knew well, where I had good friends: Afghanistan. Now I have lost contact with those Kurds; I suppose they are still fighting and teaching their children to fight for independence. And I regret not having accepted their invitation, having missed my one chance to be a guest in the house of General Barzani no less, in the mountains of Kurdistan.

At the University of Tehrān there were other Kurds, different from the ones in my class. Both groups were from Iraq. My classmates were highly conscious of the problems of their people, and active in support of the Kurdish cause; they stayed in a residential college, had little money to spare, and lived frugally. The other group of Kurdish students came from families who had been obliged to flee from Iraq. They had been welcomed and given special treatment by the Shāh, who had a policy of helping the Kurds in the neighbouring country in order to ingratiate himself with his own Iranian Kurds, and keep things more or less under control in Iran. The sons of these families would turn up at the university behind the wheels of impressive cars. They formed a close-knit group, looking out for each other, and were the rivals of an Arab group made up of Syrians, Jordanians and non-Kurdish Iraqis. The leader of these Kurds was a tall, blond, corpulent young man with wavy hair and a big moustache; he wore flares, drove a metallic-green BMW and was the boyfriend of one of the girls in my college. The girl was Iraqi but not a Kurd, which meant that their love was doomed from the start. It was a non-stop drama, and the rest of us followed its developments day by day. The rivalry between the Kurds and the Arabs came to a head from time to time in well-planned fights which took place in the entrance hall of the Faculty of Literature. All through the other faculties, whispers spread the news that at a certain time in the entrance hall of the Literature building, war was going to break out. Long before the appointed hour, the atmosphere in the corridors was palpably different. As the moment drew nearer, the entrance hall would fill up, students taking their positions on one side or the other according to which group they belonged to or supported. Naturally, as a friend of the leader's girlfriend, I was on the Kurdish side, like the rest of the girls from the college. Then the contestants arrived and stood in groups behind their respective leaders, who came forward to the centre of the hall to negotiate. If they could sort out their differences verbally, everyone went home and that was that. If not, they laid into each other, and when they were all bloody and bruised, the girls would patch them up and make a big fuss of them. Both groups had their own girls, and every member received the same tender care. Once the ceremony was over, we all went home content, discussing the situation. The Kurds in my class had no time for this kind of frivolity, and preferred to study: they had more serious problems to worry about.

With Karim, our Kurdish friend from the hotel, we visit a mosque next to his house, in which one of the sons of Ali is buried (Ali the Prophet's cousin and son-in-law, the Sword of Islam). There is an area on the left containing framed photos of young men and red flags on poles driven rather haphazardly into the ground: they represent the martyrs of the Revolution and the war against Iraq, who are buried there. Since it's a holiday, families have spread blankets on the ground and are having picnics in the midst of the graves, the photos and the flags. As is customary, they have come to spend the afternoon in the company of their dead, and the cemetery is filling up: there is a lot of weeping, but people are eating and laughing too; the children run around, and life goes on. Irene tells us about the husband of the cleaning woman she used to employ in Tehrān: he realised that the growing number of martyrs was creating a new demand, and came up with a special tin frame for photos of the deceased to be placed beside the graves. With the Gulf War he became a very rich man indeed.

The mosque is packed, but we can move around freely without any problems thanks to the *chādor*s and Bahram, who, being Iranian, does all the talking. We women follow a few steps behind him, as is fitting. There is not a single foreigner to be seen, which makes things somewhat easier. We look like tourists, but Persian tourists from Tehrān, and we can even take photos without arousing suspicion.

The door of the mosque is decorated with thousands of tiny mirrors on a surface like honeycomb, and shines so brightly you can't look at it. This door and the two slender minarets decorated from top to bottom with glazed tiles are reflected in the octagonal pool at the entrance, where the faithful wash themselves. As their movements disturb the surface, distorting the image in the water, it comes to resemble one of Gaudí's buildings.

Over dinner with our Kurdish friend, we have an easy and pleasant conversation. At the end of the meal I find myself thinking about this boy: just nineteen, married, and about to become a father; dignified, and able to keep up an interesting conversation with four people much older than himself who have seen a lot of the world. I reach the conclusion that these people must have some kind of ancestral wisdom, nothing to do with universities, be they Islamic or non-Islamic. An innate sense of how to live. We say goodbye warmly, addressing him as a brother and thanking Allah for having given us the chance to enjoy his company. We will have many more opportunities to appreciate this aspect of Iran: calm, reserved, austere and respectful; a land where time flows like a curtain of cool water, where the rare shady places are all the more welcoming, the fruits of the desert oasis especially sweet and the finely worked mosaics doubly brilliant among the adobe ruins. This is the gentle, silent face of Islam the newspapers don't talk about, the faith of men and women of goodwill.

Back at the hotel we make plans for the next day: up at seven for a day at the bazaar.

7 April

Kāshān

*E*ARLY in the morning I hear the muezzin's cry and get up to look out of the window. The adobe walls of Kāshān's houses look like copper in the light of dawn. Always visible, the snow-covered mountains seem very close. Storks are standing guard on the city's domes and minarets, one leg folded up, the other resting on a turban-like nest.

Kāshān was founded by the Sultaness Zobeida, the wife of Harun el-Rashid, who figures in *The Thousand and One Nights*. The city lies just to the west of the great salty desert, in the middle of a fertile oasis full of fruit trees. Wheat and cotton are grown here, but the main crop is the white mulberry, which for centuries has harboured the silkworms that made the city's textile industry famous.

We are drinking tea in the bazaar after two hours of wandering through the lanes full of shops and buying pairs of Kāshān slippers, which are famous throughout Persia. Back in 1874, Rivadeneyra, the Spanish Vice-Consul, wrote that: '. . . generally they were made out of a kind of piqué, but the sole was composed of pieces of blue cloth bound together with twenty or thirty catgut strings, passing through the middle of each piece'. They are available in crochet or fabric, and they adapt to the shape of your feet, fitting as closely as gloves.

These days some of them come with rubber or plastic soles. Dealings with the retailers are calm and courteous, almost hushed. There is no hard bargaining or haste; Bahram does the talking, and it's an education for us Westerners to see how the sale is negotiated. For the old, white-bearded market vendor who recites Omar Khayyām as he unfolds pieces of silk, the presence of a tourist in shorts whose sole aim is to get something for ten *rials* less must be particularly grating. It dispels the charm and hardens the vendor's attitude, encouraging him to double his price next time. Since no foreign tourists have been here for many years, we have the chance to see a relaxed Iran, getting on with its business.

Tired after so much walking and looking at things, and totally disoriented from hours of wandering through twisting streets out of the sun's reach and full of neon signs, but without names to refer to or a thread to unwind, nothing but a shop reappearing maybe – Is it the same one? Yes! It's the same vendor! – we collapse onto the carpeted floor of a tea-shop. Three times in the course of the morning I remember seeing the same shop selling white, starry cotton flowers heaped in great piles around a lean, dark-skinned man with a white beard, wearing a loose-fitting pink shirt. Sitting on the raised floor of his little booth with his legs crossed, he looked like a saint on an altar decorated with flowers or covered with snow.

We put down our parcels, adjust our *chādor*s, and look around: we are in a *saraī*, or covered square, its high Gothic dome decorated with mosaics and illuminated and ventilated by polygonal skylights, one in the middle, the others on the sides, through which we can see the sky. A ray of sunlight shines in through the skylight on our right and onto a saucer of tea a man is lifting to his mouth, the reflection illuminating his face. It is customary to sip tea from the saucer little by little so as not to burn oneself. The air is cool in the semi-darkness. Carpets are stacked up on the ground, hanging from the walls and on display. Some of the men are talking business; others are relaxing, like us, sitting on the carpets in the tea-shop. We eat the local dish, *ābgūsht*, a stew made from meat, chickpeas and fat from the rumps of sheep. The stew is served very hot in a single pot, to share. Each person mashes it up in their bowl with a kind of pestle, until it turns into a thick paste. It's the standard meal here for workmen, porters and merchants.

In the afternoon we continue to make our way through the bazaar, visiting a carpet designer famous throughout the country. His workshop is on the first floor of another *sarāī* which is on two levels, in the open air; it's square and has no balustrades. We find him sitting at a drawing table surrounded by rolls of paper, pencils, paints and strips of graph paper. His father and grandfather before him were carpet designers, and he shows us several Persian and English books on carpets featuring his designs. Weavers commission original drawings from him, and he sells them exclusive rights. He is a cultivated and distinguished-looking man: tall, slim, no moustache, very blue eyes, dressed like a European in brown trousers and a striped shirt. His hands are extremely fine and delicate. Bahram draws my attention to a photo of an athletic young man hanging on the wall. He tells me that this man was an Olympic wrestling champion who died at a very young age, for political reasons.

Bahram is unable to finish the story because two men come in and we have to step aside to make way for them. I later saw the same photo in various places in the Tehrān bazaar, and was sorry I hadn't remembered to ask Bahram for the details of the wrestler's story. His face surprised me because he didn't have a moustache or beard, for clean-shaven men are rare in Iran. I took it to be a sign of distinction. Of all the men I have seen on this trip, only four have been clean-shaven: Mr Goldar, the owner of the orchid hothouses in the north; Agha-yé Doktor, who appears later in this book; the carpet designer; and the wrestler in the photo. Later I found out that the young man in question was a famous *pahlavan*, or traditional Iranian athlete, trained in the *zurkhané* ('houses of strength'), who became a national hero after his death in 1968, possibly at the hands of the Shāh's secret police, the notorious SAVAK. The *zurkhané* date back to pre-Islamic times, and since the Islamic conquest they have been the symbol of national resistance, against Islam at first, then Sunnism, and finally the Shāh.

The men who have come into the workshop are father and son. The father is wearing a dark European-style suit with a white shirt but no tie (ties have disappeared from the male wardrobe since the Revolution), and the son is carrying an attaché case. After the customary elaborate greetings, the young man places the case on the drawing table, opens it and as if by magic, produces an extremely fine and smooth silk carpet. They are delivering it to a merchant in the bazaar, and although the reason they have come by is to pick up another design they have ordered, they take the opportunity to show the designer how beautifully the carpet turned out. For exclusive rights to the design, they paid two hundred and fifty thousand *rials*; in today's Iran, that is a lot of money.

The designer offers to take us to his home, and we climb into his new Paykan, which is parked in the sun outside the bazaar. He lives in a new two-storey house with a garden. We take off our shoes in the entrance hall, and the designer's wife and sons receive us in a room whose floor is completely covered with carpets. They give us cushions to sit on and the boys serve tea with delicious sweets and a melon sliced up on a plate, ready to eat. The wife is young and pretty; she is wearing a *chādor* of fine cotton print, white with blue flowers. Although it covers her head, the way she has arranged it over her shoulders and tucked behind her elbows lets us see that she is wearing a modern knee-length dress underneath it, with a discreetly descending V-neck and a gold chain. She is perfectly at ease, agreeing with her husband; they laugh together, and the atmosphere is relaxed. There is no talk of relatives in other countries, or visas, or children studying at American universities. We talk about carpets and our host's new drawings; he shows us a book containing the most famous designs of recent years. We recognise a carpet with two rows of birds resting on two bare branches, whose shadows fall on the plain background as if light were shining on them from the upper left corner. We saw this one, the real thing, hanging on the wall of a shop full of carpets in Tehrān, and even at the time we were struck by its simplicity and the complete lack of symmetry in its design. The eldest son, when he is not preparing or serving tea, sits with us and eats sweets. A girl, who is younger, sits on her mother's lap, while other children run up and down the stairs. They show us carpets the wife has made in her spare time, using her husband's designs. These ones are not for sale; they're being kept to hand down to the children, or for emergencies. They are exquisite. The father and son unfold them one by one, seven of them maybe: out of storage, unused, and signed. We admire them from close up, and from a distance; we touch them and look at their reverse sides. It's essential to look at the back, because if the carpet is good the design will show up with perfect clarity, as with embroidery.

They tell us that orders for designs have started to come in from China, where hand-knotted carpets as beautiful as the Iranian ones are now being made.

When you enter the world of carpets in Iran, you can end up going mad. You certainly end up disoriented, because each new carpet is more beautiful than the one before, with a finer design, smaller knots, a more natural sheen. The colours are special: sky-blue, orange or yellow backgrounds behind interlaced flowers. The explanations are always rather confusing, and there is no way to clarify them. This is understandable when dealing with a merchant who is determined to sell his carpet whatever it takes, but here, among the carpets we are looking at, there are some as smooth as a glove, and others that are stiffer; I'm curious about the difference, because I have often heard that you should be able to scrunch up a good carpet with one hand. They tell me that all these carpets are of the same quality, but some have been washed and others haven't. I ask them if they are going to wash the others, and they say no, there's no need. I want to know why only some are washed, but there is no clear answer. I'm thinking: this is what happens in the bazaar, you can never get a straight answer – it drives you crazy!

With time, you learn that the best way to keep your footing on this perpetually shifting ground is to relax and enjoy it rather than persisting in the search for a logical, coherent and reasonably accurate explanation of things. Everyone has their version, and there is always an answer – no-one admits to not knowing. But it's any old answer, so you can never really be sure that what you have been told is correct. Then there is the difficulty of the language, and the enduring cultural barrier, which you never really get over. Even if the language problems seem the same when travelling in Europe, there is never this perplexity. Back when we were staying in the house beside the Caspian Sea, right on the water, I was assured that the water was fresh, as if it were something everyone knew, and it was left at that. One person said it, the others agreed, and what did they care whether the water was salty or fresh? What was the big deal with the water anyway? I was perplexed by this certainty, in contradiction to what I believed, and later I went outside and walked down to the shore, intending to test the water like a Doubting Thomas. But it was so murky and grey, with so much foam and filth in it, that I let the handful I had scooped up pour out between my fingers. If I had drunk it, as well as settling the question, I would have been able to attribute my subsequent case of the runs to the contaminated waters of the Caspian.

Another thing you can't be sure about in Iran is whether people are telling you what they *really* think, because they have a thoroughly theatrical attitude to life. They are always on stage, always acting, and are trained to do so from a tender age. This training has been handed down for centuries and is very much a part of Iranian life. It's a stratagem for protecting private thoughts and feelings, and has come to be a permanent institution, with a name of its own: it is known as *ketman*. This is how Gobineau defines it in his book *Religions and Philosophies of Central Asia*:

The possessor of truth should not expose his person, his belongings or his reputation to the blindness, the madness or the perversity of those whom God in his wisdom has seen fit to let stray into the ways of error . . . There are cases in which it is not enough to be silent, in which silence may seem to be a confession. Scruples are out of place in such

91

cases. It is not only necessary to disavow one's real opinion, one must also exploit every kind of artifice at one's disposal to ensure that one's opponent is taken in. One must be ready to make any kind of declaration as long as it pleases, to perform any rite however meaningless, to contradict one's own writings, to essay every means of deception. Thus may one obtain the satisfaction and the merit of having kept oneself and one's family safe, of not having exposed a venerable faith to unclean contact with an infidel, and finally, of having inflicted on this infidel the shame and the spiritual misery he deserves, by tricking him and confirming his errors . . . *Ketman* is a source of pride for its practitioners. It gives the believer a permanent sense of superiority over the person he is tricking, be it a minister or a mighty king; the opponent is reduced to the status of a blind fool, for whom the true path is blocked without him even knowing it exists; you may be dressed in rags and dying of hunger, outwardly trembling before the deluded power, but your vision is perfectly clear, and you tread the path of light before your enemies. You are casting ridicule upon a stupid individual and disarming a dangerous beast. So many pleasures at once!

Ketman is a behavioural strategy developed in ancient times. In order to protect heretical views and heterodox interpretations, the leaders and ideologues of Islamic sects were not averse to simply disavowing their beliefs when speaking in public so that nobody could discover the ideas they really espoused. The practice of *ketman*, long a necessity for survival, has developed over many centuries, and is not only tolerated, but has become an essential part of Iranian behaviour. It's a permanent game. 'Saying something is white when it's black, laughing on the inside while maintaining a solemn exterior, hating while showing all the signs of love, knowing something and pretending not to: all this leads to an overestimation of one's own cleverness', writes Czeslaw Milosz in *Captive Thought*. To come off well in this game, you need to be a good actor.

Thinking about *ketman* reminds me of a friend, Dr Kasimi, a professor in the Faculty of Literature at the University of Tehrān and the host of a cultural programme on Iranian television. Before anyone had realised the Revolution was drawing near, he used to tell me how he admired the Spanish, because although they were dominated by the Arabs for longer than Iran – eight hundred years, almost a millennium – they hadn't adopted their alphabet or converted to Islam. He was a very Iranian young man, the only son of a cultivated couple, and not in the least Westernised. He had studied in Iran, and spoke to me with enthusiasm of Unamuno and Julián Marías. I have been told that after the beginning of the Revolution he appeared on television, like many other eminent Iranians, proclaiming his faith and recognising the error of his ways. I am sure he did it under duress, so as not to have to flee the country or end up in Evin, the prison on the outskirts of Tehrān, from which many never returned. I thought how terrible it must have been for such a dignified man to play that role in front of the whole country, but then I remembered *ketman*: inside, Dr Kasimi was intact, he was doing what he had to do in those circumstances, saving himself and his thoughts for better times.

Islam is a highly contradictory topic in Iran. The Iranians can't stand the Arabs, and the hatred goes back hundreds of years. The Arabs were colonists in Persia, which had been the home of a major civilisation, with its own religion, Zoroastrianism, its own language, Pahlavī, and its own cuneiform script. Fārsī, as the Persian language is called today, is derived from Pahlavī, which, like Sanskrit, is a member of the Indo-European family, and emerged from ancient Persian, the source of all present-day Indo-European languages. It's completely different from Semitic languages like Arabic, but because of the colonisation, Persian acquired many Arabic words and came to be written with Arabic characters. Iranians are offended if anyone makes the mistake of lumping them together with the Arabs. They consider themselves to be of a superior race; they think of themselves as Aryans. The last Shāh tried to exploit these feelings to involve the people in the revision of their history, claiming that Persian nationhood did not begin with the *hejrat*, when Mohammed fled from Mecca to Medina (AD 622, the year Muslims begin to count from in their calendars), but with the foundation of the Persian Empire two and a half thousand years ago. In 1971 he celebrated the birth of the Empire with great pomp in Persepolis, and in 1975 he ordered that the calendars be changed: in one day, the date went from being 1354 to 2535. All the calendars and schoolbooks had to be reprinted to incorporate the new vision of history and the new dates. The Shāh's idea was to reduce the power of the mullahs, to distinguish Iran from the Arab nations, and to restore the grandeur of the Empire. To take an example, in 1981, the Arab world was in the year 1402 (according to the lunar calendar counting from the *hejrat*), and the Western world was approaching the end of the second millennium, but Iran, if not for the Revolution, which took the country back to 1360 (according to the solar calendar, still counting from the *hejrat*), would have been in the year 2510. The mullahs could not accept these delusions of grandeur, arguing that Iran already had Shi'ism to distinguish it from the rest of the Islamic world.

Returning to the hotel, I think to myself: two afternoons in Kāshān, two unforgettable afternoons. We decide to leave for Ardestān before nightfall.

7 April

Ardestān

WE slept in a nice, clean, well-run hotel, less pretentious than the one in Kāshān. It was built during the time of the Shāh as part of a chain of small hotels designed for medium-sized cities, passed over by the international chains.

While we're having breakfast in the hotel, a pair of little blond boys with very white skin appear, followed by a couple speaking French and a Persian man. They are the first foreigners we have come across, so we're curious. We go up to their table and begin a conversation. They are passing through, travelling in a camper-van, and have come from India. Since they were only given a two-day visa to cross the country, they decided to hire a driver in Kermān; hence their Iranian companion. The woman, who is wearing khaki trousers and a khaki shirt, has her head and shoulders covered with a large white shawl.

We get to the Friday mosque before nine. Every city has its mosque for Friday, the festive day of the Muslim week. The sun is already powerful, the sky a spotless blue. The houses of Ardestān are made of adobe, like the mosque. Everything the eye can see at ground level is ochre or yellow, except for a couple of vivid green poplars emerging from behind roofless walls. The colours are intense at this time of the morning, and the dome of the mosque stands out against the sky, ochre on blue. We go inside the mosque, and are impressed by its sobriety, an invitation to prayer and meditation. The sun shines into the interior courtyard, but it's cool in the shade, under the ogival arches. Three men are sitting cross-legged in a corner, on carpets, engaged in quiet conversation; they look small seated at the base of the bare walls. Another man is contemplating the sunny area in the courtyard. There is nobody else about, and we can hear birds singing in a garden nearby. We wander for a while, absorbed in our own thoughts, until two young students suggest we go up onto the terrace for the view over the surrounding countryside. A narrow staircase takes us up onto a surface made up of humps, like the backs of giant camels standing side by side. The sudden brightness blinds us, and it takes us a few seconds to realise we are standing beside a huge dome, without mosaics or colouring, all in plain brick. Here colours are superfluous, just as words were inside.

Terraces in Iran are accessible and interesting. They are like an extra, uneven floor, without balustrades, on top of the vaulted roofs. From the terrace, you can see all the other houses and gardens, the comings and goings of the women and children in the interior courtyards, and the tops of the trees. It is customary to go up onto the roof to enjoy the sunset or the cool of a night full of stars.

After our visit to the mosque, we continue on our way to Nā'īn. All I know about Nā'īn is that it has given its name to a superior kind of carpet.

This is the heartland of Iran, sober and austere. Contrary to what one might imagine from *The Thousand and One Nights*,

Persia is a country in which colours do not abound. Most of the men and women dress strictly in black, and the villages are the colour of the desert, except for the domes and minarets of the mosques, and even they are not always coloured. There are no gilded slippers, or extravagant turbans, or strings of beads, or brightly coloured fabrics shot with threads of gold. Only the women of the nomadic tribes that you see in the markets of Esfahān and Shīrāz wear coloured garments. You might imagine that behind these walls there are well-guarded harems, enveloped in veils and sumptuous cloths. But no, behind these walls there are normal families. In each village, they opened their doors and offered us tea, shade and company. The most secret thing behind the walls was the skill in the hands of the women knotting fine carpets; the most colourful, the balls of wool they were using. And everywhere, the same kindness and courtesy, especially in dealing with older people, both men and women, for whom the Persian language, which sounds so lovely in recitations of Hāfez, reserves a specific register and codified expressions of respect.

Except in Tehrān, which is another world, the women of almost all Iranian households knot carpets, providing some extra money for the family. They finish one a year, or two, or a half, depending on the size of the carpet and the number of women and girls in the house.

The houses here have a system of ventilation based on wide prism-shaped chimneys with openings in the sides. Some of these structures have bulbous forms and curved orifices: they are so complicated they look like architectural ornaments. The building material is invariably sun-dried brick, as is normal in arid regions subject to extreme heat. It is April, and at midday in the streets of Nā'īn the heat is unbearable.

Today is Friday. Tomorrow Bahram has to work in Tehrān, so we should think about heading back. We decide to return to Kāshān via a back road, and stop along the way in Natanz, where a football match is under way on the square in front of the Friday mosque. The Muslim festive day is nearing its end; the sun is already going down, but the weather is pleasant. On a corner of the square there is an enormous tree, with a branching trunk and large roots. Children are watching the match, perched on a row of columns in front of the mosque. The players are young and good-looking, enjoying themselves on the makeshift pitch. Two boys of about seventeen chat with us and take us to see the ruins of an ancient Zoroastrian fire temple behind the mosque. On the way through a garden, one of the boys picks some almonds from a tree; they are green and still very small. He blows into his cupped hands to remove the sticks and leaves, then offers us the almonds on his spread palms. Time comes to a standstill. Toni Catany sees some flowers shaped like tulips, with red and white striped petals, and says that his mother has flowers like that in her garden in Mallorca, and that they are called wanderers because they come up in a different part of the garden each time. The boys tell us that in Iran they too have a name that refers to this surprising characteristic: they are called restless devils. They pick a few flowers to give us. And so the conversation and the afternoon unfold. We talk about their studies. They are in the last year of high school, and next academic year they will go to university. They are surprisingly modest and gentle in their manner for strong, handsome boys of seventeen, but they are also curious and have time to spend talking to people who have arrived from somewhere else on a Friday afternoon. It strikes me there must be so few opportunities for contact with the outside world in a village in central Iran today, that the boys want to make the most of our presence. All that is left of the Zoroastrian temple are four completely nondescript walls, but they gave us something on which to build our encounter.

The mosque in Natanz has a beautiful door, decorated with blue mosaics, and a conical blue and white cupola. On the right, as if guarding the door, stands a solitary minaret, which is also decorated. We end the afternoon sitting on the roots of the enormous tree in front of the door of the mosque, watching the football match, sharing our seat and the shade with a mullah.

The mountains surrounding the village rise steeply and their peaks are covered with snow. On the nearest summit, there is a Temple of Silence where the Zoroastrians used to leave their dead to be devoured by birds.

We say goodbye to all the football players and decide to have something to eat. On the way we are stopped by an old woman with a blue chequered *rūsārī* and a floral *chādor* in the same colours, who is carrying a load of flat bread. She talks with us, looks Irene and me up and down, and compliments us. Since we have a bit of a complex about our *chādor*s, we're not sure if she's being serious or joking. We sit down in a very humble *chāykhūné*, or teahouse, where a friendly old man serves us tea. We take the opportunity to buy bread warm from the oven and fresh cheese, which we eat while the old man tells us about his life and how the years since the Islamic Revolution have disappointed him. The walls are covered with pictures of Khomeinī. There are portraits of the Revolutionary leaders in every place of business in Iran, just as before the Revolution there were photos of the Shāh with Farah Dība, and before that, of the Shāh with Soraya.

Leaving the mountains behind, we enter a desert of rounded hills and dry shrubs. We are taking a secondary road, heading for Kāshān the back way. The asphalt surface is smooth and the white line down the middle is impeccable. Not a car to be seen. We bypass Kāshān and keep going towards Tehrān. After nightfall, as we approach the city, we see a cupola and four slender minarets decked out with little red neon lights. It's Khomeinī's tomb, which we passed on the way out. From a distance it looks like a fairground, except there are no Ferris wheels or merry-go-rounds.

Back at the house, while we are unpacking and getting ready to go to bed, Bahram's half-sister, who lives with Rave, turns up with her husband and children. She is the one who is leaving for Australia, and she says that everything is going smoothly; there is already somebody interested in buying the apartment, and the sale will be finalised before the end of the week, *enshā'allāh*. She is a young, attractive woman, pleasant and witty, who almost always wears red under her *chādor*, with a skirt, a lowish neckline, sheer stockings and high heels. The Iranian chapter of her life is drawing to a close, and she is very excited. She has to tell someone all about it, and that's why she has come. In her mind Australia is paradise, and although she is a bit apprehensive, she is sure they will be fine. In any case, there are bound to be opportunities for a clever, hard-working woman like her. At the moment she has a job as a secretary in Tehrān. She doesn't speak English, but the Australian government provides free classes, and she knows she will be able to learn the language quickly. The children will be fine too, because as well as free education, the government will give them an allowance for each child. And her husband? If he shapes up, good; if not, too bad for him. The husband is a plumber, and makes a living doing odd jobs around the place. He's a good man: easy-going, phlegmatic, tall and nice looking, but a bit simple. He seems to be totally at the mercy of his wife, and listening to her he smiles, agreeing with everything she says. It's patently clear that unless he's very careful, she'll leave him in Australia. But if they are all happy, what does it matter? He'll come back to his country, which is where he really feels at ease. He'll go back to being a plumber, and at Nō Rūz he'll watch the videos his wife and children send him from Australia. In the afternoons he'll get together with his relatives and friends; they'll smoke a few pipes of opium together, eat and drink, and finish up, as always, reciting Hāfez. The talk comes round to Rave and the girl again, and I go off to bed. I can hear them whispering until I fall asleep.

103

April

Tehrān – A meal at María's house – The university and
the residential college

*T*ODAY we have been invited to have a meal with a group
of Spanish women who are married to Iranian men and
live in Tehrān.

Over breakfast, as we arrange to meet up in the north-east of
the city, which is where our friends live, I discover what they
were talking about in whispers last night. During our trip to the
south, things have changed at Rave's house: there has been a
major turnaround, to say the least. In our absence, a man who
lives a few blocks down the street came to ask for Bubu's hand
in marriage. When they told me, I was taken completely by surprise, but I don't know if it was like that for them too. I would
never have thought that Bubu could get married. But I did
notice they were very excited yesterday when they were talking, because from now on they have another variable to consider: Bubu's wedding, maybe. The man is a rich merchant
from the bazaar, where he has a button shop. He came to put
the question on behalf of his son, who also has Down's syndrome. There must have been something going on already,
because when they told me I remembered that the first day we
saw Bubu by the Caspian, or maybe it was the day we went to
eat at her house, her cousins were teasing her, and she blushed,

went quiet, and lowered her eyes, hiding a mysterious smile. There must have been something going on, because Bubu went out every day to buy bread from the bakery on the corner. Bubu is a pretty girl, at least I think so, now that I know her better and have become fond of her. She is always very neatly and smartly dressed; she is also very confident and sure of her charms. But has the merchant's son been spying and seen her without her *chādor*, through a window or on the terrace? Or has he simply fallen for the girl with bread emerging from the folds of her *chādor*, whom he passes in the street every day on his way to the bazaar? It could also be a convenient arrangement, made by the families. The merchant has obviously been assuring them that his son is a fine match, not a good-for-nothing, telling them he works in the shop in the bazaar, counting buttons, and doing it better than anyone. He makes little piles of twenty-five, then puts them into boxes. He's the merchant's only helper, now that the other sons have gone abroad to study business administration. The merchant says that if the marriage goes ahead, he'll do up an apartment in the building where he lives, which he owns in its entirety, so they'll have all they need. He even said that Rave could stay with them. But he also mentioned the possibility of having Bubu sterilised so they don't have children. She'd just have her tubes tied. He says the boy is in love. They have been talking about it for a while, and when they found out about the sale of the flat and the possible move abroad, they decided to speed things up and make the marriage proposal. I don't know if Bubu was present during this conversation, sitting in a corner of the sofa with her pink angora sweater, her necklace of coloured beads and her broad, pearl-coloured fingernails. But I know it must have been a serious discussion, conducted quietly and respectfully, as always in

Iran when important affairs are under consideration, with frequent recourse to forms of polite address and invocations of
Allah, invariably Great and Generous: *Allāho Akbar!*

Going out into the street, I feel elated. Life seems marvellous as I walk through the dingy early-morning streets of
Tehrān, before the sun has started to beat down and make the
scarf stick to my head. I can feel a cool wind from the mountains on my face. As I go down what used to be Pahlavī, then
Mosadeq Avenue, now Valī-yé Asr, heading south, the trees
seem greener and taller, and the sky behind them, contrasting
with their leaves, seems even bluer than the sky over the
steppes of Central Asia, my favourite sky. I'm striding lightly
down the avenue, going nowhere in particular, thinking about
the merchant's visit to Rave's house.

Imagining the merchant, I am convinced he must have
white hair, cut very short, two or three days' growth of
whiskers, white as well, and a round head like a bristly billiard
ball, with a bump for a nose. His eyes are small, restless, glit-
tering, and almost hidden among folds of skin; his body is
barrel-shaped and he wears a black suit and a white shirt buttoned up to the top, with the corners of his unstarched collar
pointing skywards as if they are trying to poke him in the chin.
He is wearing brown shoes and white socks.

Since I have the whole morning free until lunch, I think:
why not go for a walk around the University of Tehrān and
have a look at my old residential college? I walk all the way
down what used to be Pahlavī Avenue to Ferdōsī Square, and
then head right along what used to be Shāh Rezā Avenue, the
one that divides the modern part of Tehrān from the old part,
until I get to the fence that surrounds the university campus. I
pass through the main gate and bump into the statue of

Ferdōsī, seated wearing a turban and surrounded by birds, and I greet him like an old friend. The gardens of the campus are full of building materials and machinery; new buildings are going up, and it's all rather cramped. That feeling of wide open space between the library and the university mosque is gone. During the exam period students used to walk up and down there, holding a book, trying to memorise it. I remember being surprised by the study methods of the Iranian students: as the exams approached, the avenues of the campus, Farah Park and the faculty corridors would fill up with boys and girls walking very seriously up and down for hours, looking at a book, then hiding it, and repeating things to themselves, looking in turn at the book, the ground and the sky. The corridors of the residential college were also used in this way day and night over several weeks. Faced with this spectacle, Veruta, the Rumanian girl who lived there, would look at me, and we'd shrug our shoulders. Though we didn't say a word, no doubt both of us were thinking: I don't believe this!

I went in through the side door of the Faculty of Literature, my old faculty, and found myself in the large entrance hall where the Arabs and the Kurds held their get-togethers. I strode across it, heading straight for the door that leads to the basement library. And there, among the books stacked on parallel rows of wooden shelves, I saw the very table at which Mr Samimi, the librarian, gave me lessons in Persian grammar in exchange for Spanish lessons. And sitting at another table, behind piles of books, was Dr Kasimi, the very one who talked with me about Unamuno and Julián Marías, who practised *ketman* when they made him appear on television and do penance for heaven knows what.

My first reaction was to hide: I ducked behind a row of

shelves to fix up my headscarf, pulling it back to let out a lock of hair so I wouldn't look so ugly. What with the passing of the years and the Islamic dress, I was sure I looked a fright. Until then, my appearance hadn't worried me at all, but in that moment I was thinking: when I speak to him, he won't recognise me; I'll have to remind him who I was and when he finally remembers, an expression of sorrow will pass over his face. When I knew him back then, Dr Kasimi must have been about thirty-five, and I was twenty-five. Afterwards, each time I came back to Tehrān for business, I would ring him up and we would meet in a restaurant, or at the university staff club. Sometimes we were joined by Dr Sherzad, an archaeologist and professor of art in the Faculty of Architecture.

Dr Sherzad had done his doctorate in Germany and published several books on Persian troglodyte architecture and its influence on Western architectural styles. In this context he had undertaken a comparative study of the work of Gaudí. Homa, my Afghan roommate in the residential college, and I used to call him Dr Parvané, which in Fārsī means: Dr Butterfly. We gave him this nickname before we got to know him because he had white sideburns, like Burt Lancaster in Visconti's film of *The Leopard*, wore a green suit, a silk sports shirt and, whenever the season permitted, a yellow pansy in his buttonhole. When he went out into the street he would put on a pair of sunglasses with rhomboidal lenses. I used to meet Homa after class and she'd say to me: "Today I saw Dr Butterfly in the corridor of the faculty: he was wearing an even bigger pansy than usual, and the bottom petal was black," and we'd crack up laughing. Laughter was cheap back then; we laughed about anything. Afterwards I found out that Dr Sherzad was very popular, and always got the most votes

when the students were choosing which professor would negotiate on their behalf with the high-level university administration, controlled by the all-powerful rector, Dr Nahavandi, personally appointed by the Shāh. Every year he used to take his
students, male and female, to do fieldwork in an arid, moun-
tainous region of Iran where there are important troglodyte
constructions. They would spend ten days there, drawing
plans, taking photos, observing and writing. Dr Sherzad was
very enthusiastic about his work.

Dr Kasimi was young back then, but he had the look of a
senior lecturer and moved with a certain gravity; he had very
dark skin, rather full cheeks, and wore his black curly hair
slicked back and shiny. He was a single man of sober habits,
and the only element of his invariably dark clothing that stood
out was a pair of black, brightly polished English shoes, like
two big beetles. He didn't have a car, nor did he have or intend
to obtain a driver's licence, so when he wanted to go to a place
where taxis wouldn't take him, he hired a car and a driver. Dr
Kasimi wouldn't have looked out of place in Gracia, the gypsy
quarter of Barcelona: he could have been one of the handclap-
pers who used to accompany the rumba singer Peret. He came
from a wealthy family, and although he had studied in Iran he
had probably done post-graduate work in the United States,
because he spoke impeccable American English.

Dr Sherzad, who came from a modest family and had been
to a public secondary school, attached a great deal of importance to appearances. Besides his spectacular clothing, he had
a fondness for cars. When I first knew him, he had a white
BMW sports car; later on, he used to drive around in a different BMW, a lurid metallic-green one; and the last time I saw
him in Tehrān, he was behind the wheel of a sky-blue Jaguar.

He was fifty and had been a professor for about twenty years; he hoped to be able to retire in two years, and was looking forward to it. In those days in Iran, after occupying a university chair for twenty years, you could retire on a full salary.

Dr Kasimi and Dr Sherzad were friends, and they shared an open, tolerant frame of mind. They never talked about religion with me, and I never asked them about it. The last time I saw them in Tehrān, when I said I was going to marry a man called Alsina, they thought it a wise choice because he was no doubt a descendent of Avicenna. There was a logic to this play on words: Avicenna, the great eleventh-century Persian scholar and pioneering doctor, is known in Iran as Al-Sina. We laughed at the coincidence.

The early years of the Revolution, when the university was closed, were too much for Dr Sherzad, and he couldn't face having to give up the flamboyant manifestations of his identity. He went to Germany. The last time I saw him was when he came to visit me in Barcelona. He was sad, dressed like anybody else, and had aged prematurely. He said he was worried because every seven months he had the anxiety of not knowing whether his contract would be renewed at the German university, where he was just another lecturer doing bread-and-butter teaching.

Dr Kasimi didn't want to leave Iran. He was ready to put up with whatever they did to him, and use *ketman* to hold onto a decent job at the university, so as to enjoy the magnificent garden surrounding his parents' house in the north of Tehrān, which they had managed to keep in spite of the Revolution. He also wanted to go on enjoying the forests, deserts and mountains of Iran: no-one could take those away from him.

Observing him from my hiding place behind the row of

shelves, I can see that he's as chubby as ever, and that his hair has gone almost white. He's wearing a close-fitting black suit and a black shirt. All he needs is a stick and a hat to be the picture of a gypsy patriarch. I'm tempted to vanish, just to slip away quietly, but then I think I'd never forgive myself for missing this opportunity, which might not ever come again. So I gather my courage, plant myself in front of his table and say, in a wobbly voice: *Salām Aghā-yé Doktor Kasimi* – Hello Dr Kasimi. He lifts his eyes and looks at me vacantly just for a second, but that second seems terribly long to me. Then his face lights up, and I almost burst into tears. He gets up, puts his arm around my shoulder, and with all his characteristic warmth, guides me out of the library, while faces appear behind the rows of books, staring at us.

"Doctor, I didn't think you could do that any more. Did you see how they were looking at us?"

"My friend, I would never have put my arm around your shoulder before the Revolution, but today is a special day, and if I have to, I'll go on television again to do penance," he says, looking at me with a mischievous smile. We go out of the faculty and leave the university grounds through the north gate, heading towards what used to be Farah Park, a couple of blocks away. There we have a long talk, sitting on a bench. When I used to come to Tehrān before, we would meet in an expensive restaurant and talk while smoking American cigarettes. "This time," he says, "we can talk while enjoying the scent of Iranian roses." Instead of 'Iran', he uses the word 'Golestān', which means 'Land of Flowers', and is also the title of a book of poems by one of the great Persian poets, Sa'dī. Iranians sometimes call their country 'the land of flowers'.

We talk about education, and how the Pahlavīs, Shāh Rezā and his son Mohammed Rezā, broke with tradition by establishing secular schools. These Western-style schools coexisted more or less harmoniously with the Islamic schools from 1906 until the last Shāh, Mohammed Rezā, decided he didn't need to worry about keeping tradition and modernity in equilibrium, and opted for an exclusively secular system. A totalitarian secularism.

Dr Kasimi tells me that since the tenth century, education in Iran has been linked to religion. The Quran attributes a fundamental importance to learning and wisdom, with almost seven hundred and fifty versicles concerning education, reflection, knowledge or observation, but fewer than two hundred and fifty about law and the organisation of society. He says that the Quran and the Hadith extol intellectual honesty and stress the obligation for all Muslims, men and women, to engage in the search for knowledge from the cradle to the grave, and to provide their children with an extensive, up-to-date education, drawing on new sources of knowledge wherever they are to be found, which may mean travelling, sometimes to distant countries. Similarly, the Quran enjoins its readers to share skills and knowledge, not to hoard them, and above all not to use them for material gains, since society should be the sole beneficiary of learning.

Thus Islam should be a medium for the transmission of knowledge, which, in turn, would promote the development of Muslim culture. According to Dr Kasimi, all this has been pointed out by a professor called Dr Ehsan Naraghi in a very interesting study of education in Iran. He recommends I read it.

The oral tradition has always been very important in Muslim education, and the traditional primary schools (the *maktab*) and institutes of higher education (the *madrasés*) based their system on a method designed to develop the memory and foster concentration, which relied heavily on reading aloud. Listening to him speak, I suddenly understand the comings and goings of the university students at exam-time, memorising textbooks. That was probably the only remnant of traditional education in the Shāh's universities, a fossilised remnant which, removed from its context, had become a bad habit.

We talk about the difficulty of getting into university. The year before the Revolution, out of 235,000 students who successfully completed secondary school, only 12.5 per cent could get a place in an Iranian university. Many were left disillusioned, with nowhere to go. The statistics showed that most of those who did get a place had been to private schools, which only rich families could afford; the public schools were overcrowded and, as the results in the university entrance exams showed, the teaching wasn't up to scratch. Also, as certain sectors of society grew richer, they began to send their sons abroad for their education. The rest of the young people were discontented, and even the university graduates, who had the privilege of being included in that 12.5 per cent, saw the best jobs going to foreigners or Iranians who had studied in another country. Only people with foreign qualifications could master the Western technologies that, in the end, controlled development in Iran as they continue to do all over the world.

In 1978 there were more than 100,000 Iranians studying abroad, and more than 70,000 in the United States. Although they came from wealthy families, many of them were radicals, and they founded the Confederation of Iranian Students, a broadly Marxist group. When the Islamic movement began to gather momentum, they set up Islamic student associations. In fact, many of the students who participated in the holding of the hostages in the United States embassy had studied in the US. That is why they spoke good English and had little trouble deciphering the documents the American diplomats had not been able to destroy.

"It's no use trying to impose reform by force, my friend, the force will always be turned against the reformer. Think about what happened in 1935, when the father of the last Shāh abolished the *chādor* by decree, in an attempt to modernise the country. There was such a reaction that many families decided to keep their daughters at home rather than letting them go to school without a *chādor*. So, at a time when girls had been integrated into the school system, they were excluded again, and the numbers of female students fell dramatically. You can't ride rough-shod over age-old traditions in the name of modernisation with nothing but dollars by way of compensation. The price to pay for this misjudgement was the Islamic Revolution."

As a parting remark, Dr Kasimi adds that revolutions are usually beneficial, because they stir things up and clean away the decay. And I think: true, but in the process they cause so much suffering . . .

Before heading off to lunch with María, the Spanish woman who has invited Irene and me to her house, I want to have a look at my old residential college in 21-é Azar Street, which runs along the western edge of the university. Since it is now a men's college I can't go in, and have to look at it from the outside, leaning against the fence that runs around the campus.

It's a five-storey, modern building, covered with glass, but the years have left their mark. Through the windows I can see rows of bunks, paint flaking off their iron frames, blankets hanging down and, in the rooms that have them, tatty Venetian blinds. My heart sinks. It used to be a sparkling-clean building, with double rooms, plenty of bathrooms, a fridge in the vestibule on each floor, a telephone on every landing, a public-address system, heating and air-conditioning. Homa and I had a spacious room on the fourth floor, with large windows facing south. The two beds were against the walls at right angles, and in the square that was left in the corner, there was a night table where we kept the radio cassette player. There was a wardrobe against one of the other walls, and in the middle of the room, a big square table, at which we studied. Homa made sure there were always flowers in the room. She also prepared the hot tea we drank every morning at breakfast; and whenever I had an exam coming up, I would come back from my classes and find a cake on the table in our room, with a note saying 'Good luck', signed Homa.

Homa's name comes from the bird in Zoroastrian mythology. She was very beautiful and exceptionally bright: next to her, the rest of us seemed dull and insignificant. She was also gentle, meticulous, obliging, sympathetic, smart and funny. She was the roommate I had been given, and that's how I thought of her at first, but with time I realised my luck, and it struck me that if I had been a man, Homa would have been my ideal woman.

I looked along the fourth floor until I found the window of the room Homa and I used to share, and before I knew it, I found myself remembering every detail of that black day in June – a day I will never forget.

It was a Thursday afternoon. The heat was suffocating, and the odour of sun-scorched bitumen was coming in through the window. I was trying to write a letter to my family, no doubt the last one for that academic year, and it was all I could do not to fall asleep over the papers on my desk. Ten months had passed since I first stepped into that room on the fourth floor of the residential college on 21-é Azar Street. Having done all my exams, the last one just two days before, I was enjoying a quiet day, thinking about how I would organise my departure, how I would pack up my books to send them to Barcelona, what clothes I would take, and what presents I would give to my friends in the college. The atmosphere was relaxed and festive. All the girls were getting ready to go home for the holidays, exchanging clothes and personal items. The place was more like a bazaar than a college: you take this, it suits you much better anyway; I'll swap you that for the thing over there. Everyone knew exactly what was in each room, and had been waiting for the end of the exams to try to get what they wanted. We were just waiting for our marks and doing our last bits of shopping, discussing projects for the future, boyfriends and families.

As I went on with my letter, I could hear voices from the adjoining room. For a while there had been noises, footsteps and knocks at the door. Thursday afternoon was traditionally given over to beauty care, because the next day, Friday, was a day off. A group of girls would get together in a room, where some would depilate their legs, or rather have them depilated, a job which involved two girls sitting on the floor holding special threads tightly between their fingers and dragging them down the legs to pull out the hairs. This was a laborious task, which could take hours, but there was no hurry. Other girls would be applying yoghurt masks, very good for the skin, so they said; or peroxiding all their body hair. Those who had already been through all this finished off by rubbing themselves down with perfumed oils, so their skin would be smooth, scented and shiny. It was a henhouse full of pantomime faces and dark bodies painted white. From a distance we might have been mistaken for a group of Indian warriors preparing for battle; but close up, smelling the scents, hearing the voices and seeing those sensual, feminine movements, it was like being in an eternal harem. Instead of damask wall-hangings there were posters of pop stars; instead of turbans and veils, curlers held in place by nets of fluorescent-green nylon.

The college was female territory: no man had ever gone beyond the reception area and the room set aside for visitors on the ground floor. Not even fathers or brothers were allowed upstairs. It was a five-storey feminine world with its rector, administrator, accountant, receptionist, cooks and plumbers – all women. The offices of the rector and the administrator were on the top floor, along with the door that gave access to the rooftop terrace, which no-one ever used for sunbathing, because they all wanted to stay as pale as possible.

I could guess what they were talking about in the room next door: boys and star-crossed love, and what they would do tomorrow, on Friday, when they went to spend the day at some relative's house with their boyfriend. There, in a corner of the garden, at siesta time, when all the relatives were feeling sleepy after eating lunch seated around a blanket spread on the ground, well away from the children's games and the old folk dozing, hidden behind fruit trees, surrounded by flowers, with the sound of water flowing and a voice reciting Hāfez coming faintly from the transistor radio on the blanket, there the boyfriend would run his hands over the girl's oiled body and get a few glimpses of it, or if he was lucky, see it all, and then the game would begin. They would kiss each other, and their naked bodies would tumble and intertwine on the grass. But no more, the rest was kept for after the wedding, for having children. If he loved her and intended to make her his wife, he would respect her until that day. If they went further, she would never marry him, or any other man. All sorts of fantasies could be realised before marriage, as long as you didn't lose your virginity. That's the conclusion I reached from those sessions on Thursday afternoons. Without the slightest reserve, the other girls would explain in detail what they did with their respective boyfriends, and each would learn from the others. The purpose of this exchange of experiences and ideas was to push sensuality and pleasure to the limit. That afternoon they must have been talking, as usual, about the impossible love affair between the Kurdish student and the Iraqi girl, while she cried and pulled at her hair. Their story was part of college life, and all the girls felt involved in it. It was at once romantic and tragic.

That Thursday I didn't want to join in the session, preferring to remain in my room with the letter in front of me, trying to concentrate and get it finished. I just went in to say a quick hello. Manigé was wearing the Christian Dior panties made of sky-blue Spanish lace a relative had sent her from Paris, which were the envy of all the other girls. She was the only girl in the college who had short hair. She was pretty, likeable and bold. She was different from the others. Everyone in the college knew it, and probably the whole university. I realised within a few days of arriving, and although I didn't understand the language, the girls made sure that it was perfectly clear to me.

Manigé had been raped in her village, in the mountains near Tabrīz, by a schoolteacher: one of those communist sympathisers, they said, who went out as volunteers to teach people in the country to read, during the literacy campaign launched by the Shāh. He got what was coming to him: he ended up in the river one night, after being beaten up by the men from the SAVAK, the secret police, omnipresent in those days, on the pretext that he was a member of the communist Tūdeh party. For proof, they had some suspicious poems, found under his mattress. They said Manigé's father and brother had also taken part in the torture of the young man.

I finished writing the letter, and while I was looking through a drawer for an envelope, I found some photocopies Manigé had left for me one day. She sometimes came to my room and talked about her enthusiasms, and her experiences with boys. She chose to tell me about these things because I was a foreigner, and she thought I wouldn't be shocked. She never said anything about what had happened in her village. She was a good student and she liked poetry. When she came to visit she brought photocopies of poems by García Lorca, which we read together in Fārsī. A friend of hers had translated them. Once or twice she told me that the girls with the headscarves, the ones who never came to the sessions on Thursday afternoons, didn't approve of her, and she was afraid they might get her expelled from the college. She said it would be a disaster for her, because she would lose her scholarship. Her parents couldn't afford to pay for her studies, so she'd have to leave university and go back to her village, which was something she definitely didn't want to do. It was clear to Manigé that she had to finish her course and perform well as a professional, if she was going to succeed in becoming an independent woman.

I was sorting through the sheets of paper Manigé had left for me, when a loud blow jolted me out of my thoughts. It sounded like a sack of sand had fallen onto the pavement from a long way up. There was silence for a couple of seconds, then the cries began. I heard the door next to mine open and the girls come rushing out from their session. I knew then that something terrible had happened. I opened my door and went along to the lift-lobby, which was packed full of girls buttoning their blouses or tying up their dressing gowns. They told me Manigé had thrown herself off the rooftop terrace. This detail left me perplexed, because I had heard her voice right up until just before, coming from the room next to mine. I was convinced that whatever had happened, it must have taken place in that room. What surprised me was how quickly they had all agreed about the terrace, and I was sure they were trying to avoid trouble. Instead of going down into the street like all the other girls, I went back to my room, shut the door and stayed glued to my chair, not even able to go out onto the balcony to see what was going on. I imagined Manigé's body down there, crushed and covered with blood, wearing her little sky-blue panties.

Still in a state of shock, before horror and anger began to tear at me, I remembered something Manigé had told me: the García Lorca poems we read together had been translated by a boy she knew. Suddenly, it was all clear. The rapist – the communist schoolteacher who had gone to a god-forsaken village in the mountains near Tabrīz to teach the peasants to read, the man under whose mattress they had found photocopied poems, the one they had tortured, killed and thrown into the river – he wasn't a rapist at all but her friend and lover. He must have been the one who translated the poems and read them to her.

Love, in spite of everything, and their interest in a Spanish communist poet, had cost them both their lives.

For quite a while I could hear cries and sobs from my room. The college had turned into an asylum for hysterical women. After a couple of hours Homa appeared, ashen-faced. Though normally effusive, she hardly said a word. She got her suitcase out from under the bed and piled all her things into it haphazardly. In went the little carpet and the white veil she used the only time I saw her pray, at the beginning of the year, and I watched her as she took down the photos she had stuck to the wall near her bed. She told me she had decided to go home early. She gave me a kiss, promised she'd write, and went.

That night, the girls didn't want to sleep in their rooms. There was a mass shifting of mattresses into the public rooms on the ground floor. Provisional dormitories were tearfully set up. They told me that the staff were handing out valium and that the police were asking the standard questions. I felt alone and devastated, thinking about the stigma of rape, which Manigé would never have escaped in such a society, even though it was based on a lie. I didn't want to sleep downstairs in the midst of that mass hysteria. I preferred to be on my own.

On my way up to the north of Tehrān, where I am going to have lunch with the Spanish women, I buy a postcard and send it to Homa, who now lives in New York. 'Dear Homa', I write. 'I am in Tehrān. I have just been to see our college, and I saw the window of our room. Your sudden departure left so many things unsaid. I feel I need to see you again.' I remember the day we were both lying stretched out on our beds listening to a Beatles cassette someone had sent me, with a song that went: 'because the sky is blue it makes me cry y y y y y . . .' When she heard that, Homa sat up and said: "If we had to cry every time the sky is blue here, we'd never do anything else." That song had me spellbound, I thought it was so lovely: I could have killed her. But after a moment we started to laugh and that was the end of the incident. What really moved her were sugar-sweet Indian songs, all about love. Homa and I wore tight jeans or mini-skirts, and platform boots. That's what most of the girls wore in the streets of Tehrān in the 1970s, north of Shāh Rezā Avenue.

The luncheon is at María's apartment, one of six in a new three-storey building, where five other Spanish women live with their husbands and children. These women persuaded their husbands to buy a block of land in a residential area in the north-east of the city and have the apartments built there. It's a very modern building, solid and elegant, and when I arrive the workmen are still installing the lifts.

The gathering is crowded, festive and chaotic, our presence providing an excuse for all the Spanish women who live in Tehrān to get together. We laugh, talk non-stop, gesticulate, and everyone is happy. As usual, the one making the most noise is Goyita Manucheri, the current chief secretary at the Spanish embassy, whose overwhelming vitality bears all before it. She has spent the longest in Iran, and is very happy here. She was born in Burgos, in northern Spain, but spent some years in Germany, where she met her husband, a tall, lean, serious Iranian Kurd, a Persian Don Quixote. Just as I always see Bahram in my mind's eye as an oriental gentleman, wearing a turban and a damask frock coat, I see Merdat with a helmet, armour and a lance. Goyita's expansive personality is

123

matched by her rounded physique, covered by a spectacular Islamic uniform (she is not one to be put off by difficulties): a black satin overgarment down to her feet, with elephants embroidered in gold thread down the sleeves from shoulder to wrist. On Goyita's arms there is room for plenty of elephants, and they glitter in the sun.

The women have prepared a delicious meal of Persian dishes. As we eat and laugh at their tales of adventure, we drink wine, which is a luxury, and gives the meal a flavour of transgression in this country where alcoholic drinks are forbidden by Quranic law. They talk about what life was like during the war between Iran and Iraq, with the bombing, the alerts, the fear. Now that it's all in the past, they joke about it. The Spanish embassy rented a building outside Tehrān where all the Spanish citizens and their families could stay until the end of the war. Between bombing raids, Goyita went from house to house with a van to pick up families and take them to their new residence, which, so they tell me, had only one room with a door, so they had to draw up a list to make sure that each couple got a regular turn to occupy it. It seems there were moments when communal living under these conditions was far from harmonious. But today they see it as something to joke about. I imagine a big old crumbling house with a large living room full of mattresses, children running around everywhere, the women chattering away in Spanish, taking shifts in the kitchen, the men talking in Persian, stoically watching time pass, as they like to do, surrounded by big families. Goyita was awarded the Order of the Gran Cruz de Isabel la Católica for her services.

The conversation turns to the American woman who wrote the best-seller *Not Without My Daughter*. They are all convinced she wrote the book with her husband's agreement, so as to make a lot of money, and that given its success they'll be bringing out a sequel, *Not Without My Daughter 2*. I am surprised by their adherence to this explanation, which I am sure is due in part to a defence mechanism, a refusal to admit that maybe what the book says is true, as it is true that in every country in the world there are women who are mistreated. But the barrage of propaganda provoked by the book in the West has left scars: it was so massive, and there was so much money behind it. Even my fellow lunch guests have been affected, and they are privileged people in this country: they have jobs, go back to Spain each summer, and watch satellite television.

I overhear Irene talking with Goyita about the possibility of obtaining temporary visas for Rave and Bubu, to allow them to go to Spain so that Rave can be treated by Dr Barraquer. It sounds like it can be done, and the forms have to be submitted as soon as possible to speed up the procedure.

After lunch, since there is plenty of the day left, I decide to spend the afternoon in the bazaar. As soon as I leave the house I find a corner to stand on, and start yelling my destination and the price I am prepared to pay at each taxi that passes. My friends, who have a better knowledge of the taxi system, have given me the right price. If one stops, it's because he's going in that direction and has accepted the price. Everyone catches taxis like this in Tehrān. As well as the driver, there is room in each car for five passengers packed in tightly: they climb in and extract themselves at various points along the way. Men and women travel together, the women wearing *rūsārīs* or

125

*chādor*s. How is it that a woman is allowed to travel from one side of Tehrān to the other jammed up against a man with a big moustache, his elbow pressing into her kidney, and on the other side buttock to buttock with a scrawny mullah? Taxis are often the only places where young lovers can squeeze up against each other. In buses, men travel in the front part, women behind. Women and men sit separately in the rare cinemas, which show action films with gangsters sporting moustaches, whose girlfriends, instead of being platinum blondes, wear *chādor*s. In mosques, women have a special area. Taxis are a major anomaly.

It seems that respect for the mullahs is waning. Today in the taxi, as we passed a stumpy little man with thick round glasses, a brown cape and a white turban, who was signalling that he wanted to get in, the driver swerved slightly and almost made him fall into the *jūb*, the open drain in the street. Everyone burst out laughing at the way he jumped aside, and then they started telling mullah jokes. It seems to be the fashion in Tehrān.

I saw a woman out of Islamic uniform today, for the first and only time during my visit. She went past me in the street near the bazaar, wearing loose trousers and a vast, unravelling jumper, slippers and a cloth cap, all in an indistinct desert-soil colour. Her hair was cut very short, you couldn't really see it, but just a few locks showed that it was almost white. At first glance she might have passed for a man, but she was too pale, and she had no moustache. It was a woman! She looked like a beggar, but a beggar with class. Afterwards I was told she was an Argentine who had been in Iran for many years: her husband had died a long time ago and she lived on her own. When the Revolution came, she hadn't even thought of leaving the country, or wearing a *chādor*, and obviously no-one had made her do so. It must be because her body doesn't have the characteristics required in the East to provoke lustful thoughts. I have been told there is an English woman at the British embassy who shaves her head so as not to have to cover it. It seems that if there is no hair, there is no sinful attraction. That's the way things have gone since the Revolution started in '79.

It's really the men, however, rather than the women, whose appearance has changed with the Revolution. Men in Tehrān today look quite different from the way they looked during the time of the Shāh. The tie and the clean-shaven face are signs of Western civilisation, and as such have been banished. It is normal to have a couple of days' growth or a longer, well-groomed beard, a dark or grey suit, neither too new nor too well pressed, and for merchants in the bazaar, a waistcoat and a white shirt with an unstarched collar, or better still without a collar, and buttoned up to the neck. Shoes tend to be large, with uppers that can be squashed down at the heel so they can be worn like slippers. Iranian men never really took to the completely clean-shaven look, not even in the old days, and less still now. Before the Islamic Revolution, moustaches were standard: big handlebars, little Hitler-style stripes or the Stalin model. Now they all have undesirable connotations, though they're not absolutely forbidden of course. It's better to grow a beard if you're applying for a job, asking for a raise or negotiating a contract, just as Western men in such situations shave carefully, make sure their suit is well pressed and put on a tie.

This afternoon I got lost in the bazaar. I went in through a side door, towards the southern end, after having walked through narrow lanes I had never seen before, and found

myself in the section devoted to paper, pencils and other stationery. All the shops were selling stationery: streets and
streets full of paper and rubber stamps; a whole afternoon in
the midst of pencils, envelopes and erasers. I wandered
through mosques, and in each patio I thought I knew where I
was, but when I came out I was still lost. I was hoping to find
the button section, and locate the shop belonging to the merchant who lives near Rave, so I could see Bubu's suitor. I
knew that if I could get to that section I would see the boy, just
as I had run into the one-armed caviar man in a street full of
pedestrians when I ventured into the world of the black market, trying to buy a small round blue tin with a sturgeon
painted on the lid. But Allah has not willed it so today. I'll
come back.

On my wandering way through the lanes of the bazaar, I
stopped to watch a calligrapher at work. Sitting on the wooden
floor of his small workshop, at a table covered with carefully
arranged pens and ink, the man was transcribing texts in an
exquisite hand. From his pens came letters that looked like
variously coiled snakes and together they formed a sort of fil-
igree. I asked him what he was writing, and he said it was a
poem by a Persian woman, ordered by a female client. It was
about curtains and windows, but the hand was so ornate I had
trouble reading it. Like Arabic, Fārsī is written from right to
left, so their books start where ours end, on the 'last' page.
Each page begins in the top right-hand corner. In Fārsī, many
of the spoken vowels are left out when it comes to writing. The
letter 'i' is the only one that is always written. To write the 'a',
but only the closed 'a', they use the famous *alef*, the first letter of the alphabet, which has the form of a vertical pole,
except that it's never exactly vertical but always dancing, like

all the letters of the Arabic alphabet. The other 'a's are not written. The 'e' doesn't exist at all, and 'o' and 'u' are represented by the same sign, which also stands for 'v'. Learning to read in Fārsī is a fascinating and amusing adventure, each word a challenge and a surprise, a riddle to be solved. At first, when you're faced with a bunch of consonants and have to put the vowels in yourself, it seems impossible to discover what the word is. Depending on the problem, there are various ways you can try to solve it: with the repetition, combination or permutation of vowels, but of course you have to know the language well enough to recognise the word when you hit on the right sequence. Unlike Arabic, Fārsī doesn't have those accent-like signs which are placed between the consonants, near the tops of the letters, to indicate the vowels. Often it is the 'i' that saves you: the 'i's are unambiguous, you can rely on them. If you find an 'i' in a word, you know you are on a firm footing, and you won't make a mistake. As an apprentice reader of Fārsī, I hereby pay my grateful homage to the letter 'i'. When it comes to writing, the Persians have opted for economy, using no more signs than are absolutely necessary. A Fārsī text is less fancy than one in Arabic, adorned only by small dots above or below certain letters.

When I left the bazaar and went back into the streets, through a completely different gate from the one I thought I was going to emerge from, it was getting dark, and the footpaths were full of people looking for taxis, all yelling out their destinations. Tehrān is a safe city.

129

April

Tehrān – Visiting the tourist bureau – Armenians and Jews

I DON'T know what the date is any more; all I know is that it isn't Friday and I'm in Tehrān.

Before I left Barcelona I agreed to visit the National Tourist Bureau on behalf of a travel agency in Madrid. They gave me the director's card. Iran set up a large pavilion at the last FITUR tourism fair, and this means they're interested in attracting tourists, or so they told me in Madrid. Go and see what the conditions of entry into the country are, what the visa situation is, if you can move around freely, and how it's all organised.

I rang up to make an appointment, thinking that today was a good day for the visit, and they told me I could come in straight away. I went to the bureau and was received by a very young woman wearing a totally black Islamic uniform, typing at a desk. I was wearing my uniform too: beige overcoat and dark green headscarf. While I was waiting for the director to come out, she told me she was divorced and had a little girl. Her eyes were sad.

The director didn't shake my hand when he greeted me. It isn't the done thing to shake hands with a woman. He was wearing a dark suit and a white shirt buttoned up to the top, without a tie; his hair was short and he was unshaven, wearing a couple of days' growth. He was young, couldn't have been more than forty, and was the perfect image of the Islamic civil servant. I started to speak in Fārsī, which he found amusing, and the tension seemed to ease. He was pleasant, but rather surprised by my presence. Why hadn't I made inquiries in Spain before leaving? How had I got into the country? How had I got a visa? Who was I with? And so on. It wasn't normal for people to visit Iran as individuals without going through the official channels; they would have preferred to accompany me throughout my visit, and in fact he offered to look after me for the rest of my stay. I managed to get out of this by saying I only had a short time left and would be spending it with my hosts, which sounded convincing because Iranian families organise a heavy social schedule when they have a guest. My explanation seemed reasonable to him and he gave me all the information I needed. The bureau takes care of everything when there is a group of tourists: there are various itineraries and rates, and visas are part of the package, the money being paid into a bank account in Bahrain. "Bahrain? Not Iran?" I wondered. He said it without offering any explanation, and I didn't dare ask why, but I did tell him that if they wanted to attract tourists, they should put toilet paper in the hotels.

On the way out of the office, after the interview, he told me that from then on the young woman I had met on the way in would accompany me on my sightseeing and shopping trips. I saw her eyes light up and she looked at me imploringly. I thanked him for the offer, but there was so little time left . . . He left us alone together and just as I was about to leave, she told me she would be missing an opportunity to talk with another woman. I could see that she badly needed to express her restlessness, and felt shut in wearing that beetle-like uniform, but also shut inside an invisible jail, where it was impossible to relate to other people sincerely and naturally, where there was no end to acting and everything was theatre. She said she liked to read and listen to music, but it was hard to get hold of books and records (they circulate secretly in Iran), and she felt she was stifling in such a closed world. I left the tourist bureau with a heavy heart and a certain feeling of guilt. I could have made a bit of time if I had really wanted to, but right from the start, something wouldn't let me; and that something was my entrenched refusal to give myself over to the staff of the tourist bureau. I didn't want anyone checking up on me or following my every move, although my intentions were completely innocent.

I knew that the young woman would have to submit a daily report on our activities, and even if it was just a formality, the mere idea made me cross. Since I was such an atypical visitor, they didn't exercise much pressure to bring me into line; it was just a token attempt. All the same, I'm sure that if I had acquiesced they would have taken me all around the country and made a great fuss of me, in their own inimitable fashion.

When I arrived in 1973, young and bewildered, a student-cum-guide was assigned to me by the Ministry of Education for the first few days of my stay. He was a pleasant boy, curious and thirsty for knowledge. I considered his presence to be a mark of the country's courtesy and put up with it politely, although it soon became a drag. Gradually I discovered that he knew many things about me that I had never told him, and one day he confessed that he submitted a daily report to the Ministry, and that in one such report he had recorded the fact that when I spoke of the Gulf I called it the Persian rather than the Arabian Gulf, which was considered a good sign. I told him that in Spain it was always called the Persian Gulf, from

133

the very first Geography classes in primary school, and as soon as the opportunity to get rid of him presented itself, I seized it, because as well as all this he was starting to fall in love with me.

I think the people who have lost most as a result of the Islamic Revolution are the urban middle classes and the intellectuals. The rich left the country, or continue to come and go as it suits them; the rural poor live much as they always have, with their ancestral traditions, their fervour and trust in Allah, but without being scandalised by the excessive imported luxuries enjoyed by a small minority during the time of the Shāh. That luxurious way of life was favoured by the buoyant economies of the Western world and the high price of petrol. It was paraded in front of the poor, who had not the slightest chance of participating in it. The middle classes, on the other hand, were on the point of tasting the fruits of prosperity, and had already reached a reasonable level of financial comfort. Since the Revolution, the country has slipped back economically because of the Iran–Iraq war. Oil brings in less money than before, the population is growing at an extraordinary rate, and the State has stopped employing new civil servants and commissioning public works. The country has lost credibility in the rest of the world: foreign companies no longer accept Iranian credit cards, and imports can only be paid for with hard cash. All this has meant an increase in unemployment. The atmosphere in Tehrān is one of austerity and uniformity. The other big losers were the progressive professionals, the intellectuals and the artists. Although they were enthusiastic about the Revolution at the beginning, many were later imprisoned and executed during the most repressive phases. Today, those who are left struggle to get by, keeping their heads down, with little hope for the future.

Iran has changed since the beginning of the Revolution. Every family has suffered terrible blows, but stability has slowly returned, and life goes on. The very rich travel round the world and have houses in Los Angeles. The not-so-rich, with half the family left in the country trying to obtain elusive visas and the other half living abroad, struggle to get by and find their place in a world where people mix them up with third-world Arabs because they don't know any better. The poor are poorer than ever, paying tribute to the sons who gave their lives for Islam and living in resignation, with the help of the mosques. The merchants in the bazaar have profited from the disappearance of State control and competition from multi-nationals. Being good Muslims, they support the clergy with generous donations and finance the construction of schools and hospitals through the mosques. That's how they pay taxes now. The merchants are in favour of absolute liberalism in matters of commerce, it's part of their age-old struggle against the centralised state, which keeps trying to prey on them with taxes and impose foreign monopolies. For the men from the bazaar, any kind of dealing is all right, as long as the profits are shared with the community. The State has always been a dead weight.

The only way to have a window onto the outside world and Western corruption is to buy a satellite dish. The Iranian tele-vision stations are state-run and 100 per cent Islamic – the woman who presents the news is strictly clad in a *chādor* – but there are also very popular Iranian soaps, avidly followed by every housewife. A satellite dish gives access to MTV, with endless clips from Michael Jackson, Madonna and co; they can also get Hong Kong television and many other chan-nels. All this is mouth-watering for young, urban Iranians condemned to either live in a state of permanent contradiction and discontent or convert to extreme Islamic fundamentalism. So different from the simplicity and ingenuity of the young people we met in the villages of rural Iran! But that simplicity cannot be maintained with prohibitions; no-one can change the dynamic of a system running wild, equipped with invisible electronic tentacles reaching into the most remote places. Obviously, satellite dishes are not sold in shops, but if you want one and you have enough cash, they can be found. People have been saying that they will be prohibited, and in fact the newspapers have announced a ban, but Iranians laugh and joke about it. "Sooner or later someone in the West or Japan will come up with invisible dishes." For now, the dishes are migrating from terraces down into gardens and under the trees.

As I have a bit of time to spare, and the sun has been blinding me ever since I left the tourist bureau, I slip into the Armenian Cathedral on the other side of Karīm Khān-é Zand. Plunging into the darkness, it takes me a few moments to recognise the saints, virgins and crucifixes after stumbling against pews and kneelers. Heads turn at the noise, and a woman beside me puts a finger to her lips and says, "Shhh."

A saying from *Don Quixote* comes into my head: "There is nothing for it Sancho, we are up against the Church," although it's not the Church of Rome. Armenian Iranians look just like Muslims, and for that matter just like Assyrians, Jews and Zoroastrians; in the street, you can't tell the difference. I sit down in the back pew, and enveloped in silence and darkness

I can smell incense on the cool, damp air. The atmosphere starts to feel strange and rather sinister, and I find myself thinking of Bubu. Apparently Irene is putting together the papers for a visa application. I don't think it's a good idea for Bubu to leave the country: here, she knows the language and is at ease; she has her habits and activities. The best thing for her would be to marry the merchant's son. In fact, both possibilities are being considered, and I am definitely in favour of the wedding. I have made my position clear and I almost got cross this morning when Irene started telling me about the birth certificates. My head is buzzing; there are Christs and cherubs everywhere I look as Bubu's awful predicament unfolds before me. How could they take her away from her street, when she could stay put and keep going to buy bread every day, following the route she knows, stopping to talk to the neighbours who greet her affectionately. What is she going to do in the outer suburbs of some industrial European city: disoriented, frightened, shut up in a poky room on the nineteenth floor of a high-rise block among twenty identical blocks, surrounded by immigrants from other countries? Bubu bewildered in a Tower of Babel. It's because they've all gone mad, I think, mad for visas, as if the best thing that could happen to anyone is to get a visa, even if it's a visa for hell. I'm annoyed, and on the way out I trip over a kneeler again; the faces turn and I hear another "Shhh," before the sunlight blinds me once more and a white curtain is drawn in my mind, sealing away the nightmare.

The Armenians make up an important community in Iran. They came from Armenia when Shāh Abbās I (1588–1629) gave them asylum, settling near Esfahān, where the court was located, on the opposite side of the river. They founded the suburb of New Jolfā, in memory of the city they had come from: Jolfa in northern Turkey. They also built the cathedral in Tehrān and set up the first printing press in Iran. In the Tehrān telephone book there are many Armenian names: Agassian, Mardirosian, Kachaturian. The Armenians have a reputation for being cultivated and artistic. For a while after the Revolution, the only place where concerts continued to be given was the Armenian Club in Tehrān, until they were forbidden there too. When Iranian trucking magnates – all very wealthy Persian gentlemen – came to Barcelona to do business with Trabosa trailers, we took them to a concert at the Liceo if they were Armenians, and if not, we organised a big meal and did the rounds of the saucy cabarets. The Armenians stayed at the Hotel Ritz, the others at the Princess Sofía.

Another important minority in Iran are the Jews, who still have their antique shops near Ferdōsī Avenue, and their money-changing businesses. They served as middle-men in the massive transfers of money out of the country at the beginning of the Revolution. People say that during that time of uncertainty, when anyone who had money was trying to move it to a safe place, veritable mafias of swindlers sprung up around the embassies. Many foreign con men had nice summer holidays at the expense of Iranians who had entrusted them with large sums of money that never reached their destinations. By contrast, the Iranian Jews proved to be highly scrupulous and reliable; they charged a high percentage for the operation, but the money always arrived, in spite of the fact that there was no paperwork, just a verbal agreement.

Today, Toni Catany and I went round the music shops looking for Iranian music recordings, but there weren't many. Not a single woman's voice, because even the most classical female singers are forbidden. What you can find is *setar* music, played on the Iranian three-stringed instrument, and other instrumental recordings; one of the current favourites is a pianist who plays a sort of Westernised mood music, in the style of Richard Clayderman. In the shops they asked us if we had any Gypsy Kings or flamenco rumba recordings, and assured us they would buy as many cassettes of that type of music as we could bring with us on future trips. No doubt these shops serve as outlets for a busy black market.

Since returning to Tehrān we have been invited to dine with relatives and friends every night, and every night there has been a big gathering and a delicious meal. Iranian cuisine is mild; they don't use hot spices but are very fond of pickles, which they call *torshī*, made with herbs, vegetables, garlic, onions and dried limes. They keep them in jars and use them to accompany various dishes. Every Iranian housewife has her own, jealously guarded recipe. When you pass a window where the season's jars of *torshī* are sitting quietly in the sun, whiffs of wonderful smells whet your appetite. No Iranian meal is complete without *sabzī*, and rice, which is cooked in a variety of ways, from classic white rice to sweet rice mixed with finely chopped candied orange peel and all the different coloured rices, with pistachios, almonds, *serej* (the small, round, very bitter red fruit) or saffron. The rice is cooked in such a way as to leave a toasted but not burnt crust on the bottom of the pan, which comes off easily and is served separately – the *tadīg* I mentioned earlier, and I have to say again: it's delicious. Rice is served as an accompaniment to meat, which is cooked on skewers or in strips with a sauce, as in a stew. It is also served with *khōresh*: thick soup made with green vegetables and eggplant. Yoghurt, served in various ways but always salty, is rarely absent from a Persian table. The traditional drink is *dūgh*, yoghurt diluted in plenty of cold water with a little salt and chopped mint. It's very refreshing in summer.

Shopping for spices and produce in the bazaar is a delight, especially if you are able to ask the shopkeepers about the contents of each bag and can understand their explanations. Back at the house, Bahram's mother gave me a practical cooking class, and we spent the afternoon surrounded by pots. My suitcase is full of little packets containing indispensable ingredients for cooking good Persian dishes when I get back home.

Today we went to Agha-yé Doktor's house. Since our arrival, there has been talk of going to have lunch with this man, Bahram's uncle, a doctor by profession. From the tone of the conversation each time he was mentioned, I gathered that he must be an important person in the family, and a figure to be reckoned with in Iranian society, both rich and influential. Whenever there was a problem, he was the one to consult: go and see Agha-yé Doktor, ring Agha-yé Doktor to see what he thinks, ask Agha-yé Doktor if he knows anyone, Agha-yé Doktor will take care of it, and so on. In Persian, Agha-yé Doktor simply means Mister Doctor. It is customary to address men with their title or the name of their profession, even within the family.

Naturally, Agha-yé Doktor lives in the north of Tehrān, where the rich used to live during the time of the Shāh, and have gone on living under the Islamic Revolution. He greets us at the garden gate; the house is a modern, three-storey affair.

He is a corpulent man, with almost white hair, and he has neither beard nor moustache. He is wearing a double-breasted dark suit and an immaculate white shirt with a carefully pressed collar and white shirt cuffs emerging from his jacket sleeves to reveal golden cufflinks. He sports a tie with a colourful geometric design. Agha-yé Doktor is the incarnation of Iranian opulence – I mean the opulence of the old days. He looks just like the transport magnates Mr Bartomeu and I used to deal with when we came to negotiate the sale of trucks and trailers.

The doctor occupies the ground floor of the building, and since he now lives alone he has turned it into a small but comfortable and charming apartment. His wife and children are in America, having left at the beginning of the Revolution. Once he had got them properly settled in, he came back to Iran to live among his own people, where he feels at home. All in all, the Revolution hasn't caused him too much hardship: he doesn't bother anybody and nobody bothers him. He can leave the country whenever he wants to, but he doesn't even do that very often any more, it's such a performance: the wife, the children, America . . . Since he has already made his money, and is well established in his profession, why would he want to start from scratch and struggle to make his way in a foreign country that doesn't interest him particularly? Here, everyone calls him Agha-yé Doktor, the family venerates him, and he has his friends and colleagues to chat with in the gardens of north Tehrān, where the air is pure, above the pollution.

Many Iranian men who left the country at the beginning of the Revolution are waiting until they retire to come back to Iran. Their country is like a fond mother who protects and lulls them, providing them with delicious food for the body and the soul. Bahram already spends most of the year in Tehrān, and Ahmad Goldar, the owner of the orchid hothouses, has come back too. As for another acquaintance, Sohrab, Professor of Dietetics at a university in Chicago, he is waiting for the day when he too can go home. His case is typical of the situation faced by many professional Iranians who are thinking about their retirement.

Sohrab is a doctor; he studied in Italy and married an elegant and intelligent Italian woman. When the Revolution began, Sohrab was just over forty and a well-known medical practitioner in Iran; Antonella, his wife, was a translator. They stayed for a while during the euphoric phase of the Revolution, because it was a time of creative change, and many people were enthusiastic about making a new start. But things took a turn for the worse, and they decided to emigrate to America with their two young daughters. Sohrab had to learn English from scratch. He had to reach a high enough level to pass language tests before being able to sit for the exams which gave him the right to practise medicine in the States. It took him a few years to do it, but now he is a professor at Chicago's Loyola University and lives in a nice house, surrounded by trees, in one of the city's residential suburbs. Nevertheless, Sohrab is planning to go back to Iran as soon as he retires, and is counting the days of the few years left to go. The women can do what they like. If they want to go back, they can go back; if they want to stay abroad, fine. Naturally, the children, especially those from mixed marriages, have no intention of returning to Iran, and the daughters of these couples are allergic to talk of potential Iranian husbands. The fathers, on the other hand, go back to a cosy and comforting existence in the old country where, surrounded by friends and family, they talk, eat, smoke, drink and recite Persian poetry, while the mothers, sisters-in-law or aunts cook and organise everything to make life easy and pleasant.

We dined on the first floor of Agha-yé Doktor's house, where one of his nieces lived, with her husband and children. They were a nice-looking young couple. The man was wearing corduroy trousers and a checked flannel shirt; his beard was short and neat. The woman had a stunning head of dark, wavy hair. Their children, a boy and a girl, were in their teens, and the boy had one of his friends around to visit. They were wearing jeans, navy-blue Lacoste shirts and moccasins; they looked like boys from a good family in Barcelona.

The father was a professional copier of paintings, although he was sometimes commissioned to do portraits. The living room was full of paintings, side by side, as in a gallery. Here a Delacroix, there a Velásquez or a tavern scene, a hunt, a landscape – all by famous painters. He copied them out of books that people had brought him from Europe. The copies were very good, and came with elaborate gilded frames. Apparently, they are all the rage in Tehrān high society, and cost a great deal. There was no talk of visas in this family.

The dinner was delicious. There was *kashk-é bādenjūn*, one of my favourite dishes, made with eggplant and a kind of dry yoghurt. Solid and slightly sour, the yoghurt is sold in lumps in the bazaar, and looks almost like plaster. To cook it, they grate it up and make a white sauce, an excellent accompaniment to the grilled and chopped eggplants. *Kashk* is not smooth like everyday yoghurt: it has a rather strong taste and a somewhat pasty texture on the tongue.

After dinner, Agha-yé Doktor revealed his secret to us: he pushed aside a piece of furniture that was leaning against the

143

wall under the staircase to reveal a door behind which he kept all his treasures. He had been collecting them throughout his life, building up a kind of museum of personally significant objects. There were paintings, Islamic calendars from certain key years and a gold-framed picture of Ali, the Prophet's son-in-law, with his sword, the Sword of Islam; underneath, Arabic calligraphy; to one side, hand-written poems sur-rounded by ornamental borders, the uniform he wore when he did his military service, diplomas, books and various other objects. He kept specimens in jars of formalin on a shelf: a foe-tus the size of a hand, with hair and teeth, which he extracted from a soldier's stomach when he was an army surgeon – a twin brother, encysted all that time; a gigantic big toe; a dis-quieting eye . . . Agha-yé Doktor handed me each jar so I could get a better look, and when I had seen them all, that big room seemed like a chamber of horrors. Presiding over the museum was a large portrait, painted by his nephew, in which Agha-yé Doktor was seated in a white lacquered armchair upholstered with garnet-coloured velvet. He asked Toni Catany to take his photo next to this portrait, and I have kept a copy: Agha-yé Doktor is wearing the same suit, the same shirt, the same tie, and even the same cufflinks! At the time I didn't appreciate the subtlety of the set-up.

April

Tehrān – Going to get bread with Bubu

I STILL don't know what the date is, but I can feel that the end of my trip is drawing near. Entangled once again in the spider's web this country spins for me, I am pleased to find that I have forgotten all about the rest of my life.

Today, I arranged to go to Rave's house on my own after breakfast, on the pretext of taking some presents over. With a bit of luck I'll get there as Bubu is going out for bread, and be able to accompany her. Back at the house, Irene is persisting in her attempt to get hold of the elusive papers: birth certificates, photographs, permits and so on. Battling with the most rigid bureaucracies is one of her specialities. She can take them on because she handles official documents with an enviable deftness – no public servant can hold out against her. She is the scourge of ministries in Iran, Spain and the United States.

As usual, breakfast was a briefing session before going our separate ways. Irene put her papers in order, and planned her day, step by step; Toni Catany sorted out his rolls of film and checked his cameras; I looked at the map with Bahram to get my bearings. His mother was the only person who was going to stay at home, smiling and calm, with her pots, her prayers and the peace that comes from knowing that one's happiness doesn't depend on a visa.

My plans to go out for bread with Bubu fell through. When I got there, she had just returned. But Rave and Bubu were alone, and glad to see me. When Rave went off for a moment to tend her pots, I took the opportunity to ask Bubu if she wanted to get married. I couldn't understand what she said, but I saw her smile as she turned her head away, as if she wanted to hide her face; then she launched into a series of explanations, gesticulating abundantly to make herself understood, but none of it made any sense to me. Nevertheless, I could tell she had become very serious and was saying something important. I got the impression it was something she found embarrassing, but also pleasurable, to talk about.

I'm convinced that Bubu would like to get married, that she's in love and full of hope. Rave told me they're still talking it over with the boy's father. They said he came to visit them yesterday, and brought them gifts: a silk scarf for Rave and a gold bracelet for Bubu, which they showed me, happy and excited. The merchant came with his son Akbar, and they spent the whole afternoon talking, drinking tea, nibbling pistachios and eating fresh cucumber. They talked mainly about practicalities, and mentioned Allah frequently in the course of a conversation punctuated by set phrases and expressions of respect. I asked them what the boy is like, and apparently – at least according to Rave, and she is Bubu's grandmother after all – Akbar is not nearly as good-looking as Bubu, but he's a nice boy, who makes himself useful; it's amazing how easily he gets around the lanes of the bazaar, where everyone has known him since he was little.

There I was, sitting on the sofa in the dining room in front of the television screen where Michael Jackson squawks every night, with Rave and Bubu, one on either side, laughing and cracking jokes about the wedding. Bubu had gone the colour of a tomato and was hiding her face, pouting from time to time, but listening to the jokes. I was thinking: Iran is a wonderful country. I'm going to have to go back to Barcelona without having found the in-laws' stall in the bazaar, without having seen the boy, without really having any idea how it will turn out. I said goodbye, knowing I wouldn't see them again before I left Iran, and promising to come to the wedding.

April

Tehrān – Toilets and terraces

$\mathcal{A}$ CCORDING to V. S. Naipaul, who apparently came across it in an article on urban planning in the Iranian magazine *The Message of Peace*, Islamic toilets should be oriented in such a way that when using them neither the face nor the backside is directed towards Mecca. I don't know if this is true in all cases, or if it has always been taken into account, but it could well be one of the consequences of the fundamentalism that for quite a while now has been driving studies on Islamic urban planning. In any case, it strikes me as logical.

I never would have thought this topic could interest me, but never before have I had the opportunity to go into so many mosques or needed to use their toilets. I have been pleasantly surprised by their extreme cleanliness in every case. I am talking about Persian toilets, without a bowl, just a hole in the ground, the kind one finds in all public places and all Iranian homes except modern apartments in Tehrān. But even there, as well as the European-style bathroom, there is often a little room with a Persian toilet.

It's not that Iranians are essentially more fastidious than other mortals, but the Quran says that after voiding one's bowels one should always wash with water. The precept has been observed for centuries, and is part of elementary Islamic education. In all toilets, there is a tap with a hose or, in the most basic ones, a container of water which is full when you come in and should be full when you leave. There's sure to be a tap nearby. The cleanliness of the place is maintained with great care, as a spiritual exercise in purification, leaving no visible remains of any kind. Since there is no paper, bins are not required, and there are no scraps lying around.

I can confirm that all mosques, even the most humble, have separate toilets for men and women. They are very simple: the walls are earth-coloured, like all the other walls, and there is nothing inside but the black hole in the floor. It was a great relief to discover these toilets, given my condition during the trip to Kāshān and Nā'īn.

The European-style toilets you occasionally find in public places are not so clean. Generally you can make out footprints around the edge of the bowl, as many Iranians, used to the other kind of toilet and no doubt apprehensive about the idea of sitting on something cold and wet, prefer to step up onto the bowl. They say that squatting helps prevent constipation and that cold water is good for haemorrhoids, which goes to show once again how much sound advice there is in the Quran; after all, it is a compendium of ancestral folk wisdom.

While we are having lunch with some friends, they remark that soon the great heat will be here, and it will be time to move the beds up onto the terraces. A memory surfaces from the time I spent living in the residential college. In the small hours of a June morning, I happened to look out of my fourth-floor window which had a view over the interior courtyard of a city block, and was surprised to see the buildings' flat roofs covered with camp beds in which people were sleeping. They used to move their beds up onto the terraces when summer came, just as in their villages it was customary to move them out into the walled gardens when the heat was intense. In the morning I would see them wake up, stretch, and fold the mattresses over. I can't remember how the women were dressed for this communal sleeping, or even if there were women, I only remember that the men got out of bed in striped pyjamas, the same ones they wore in the street under their suits. Dr Kasimi once told me that at his house in north Tehrān it was customary to move the beds onto the terrace as soon as it started to get hot, and sleep under the stars right through the summer.

The terraces of Tehrān make up a vast discontinuous surface, on which, at the beginning of the Revolution, the inhabitants of the city gathered as night fell to chant in unison *Allāho Akbar*, God is Great. The chanting spread throughout the city from terrace to terrace until the millions of voices joining together in the darkness sounded like an overwhelming roar coming directly from somewhere deep in the earth's core. Everyone who hoped that the return of Khomeinī would gather the country's forces to bring about a necessary revolution went up onto the terraces. Not just devout Iranians, but also those who, religious beliefs aside, were opposed to the Shāh and his corrupt and repressive regime. It was a time of hope and concentrated energy, during which everybody got behind the idea of creating a new Iran. Even the dispossessed, encouraged and supported by the grass-roots clerics, decided to leave their rundown, dirty neighbourhoods in the south of Tehrān and go up to the north: an army in rags occupying the university, the avenues, the parks, marching into the city of the rich.

April

Tehrān – Going Home

ᴛᴏɴɪɢʜᴛ, or rather in the small hours of tomorrow morning, I'll be flying back home. I devoted the day to spending the last *rials* I had left. I bought more spices, some bedspreads and tablecloths (hand-printed with a traditional design using carved wooden blocks), glass knick-knacks, a pencil case with miniatures on it and an illuminated page from a book, showing a man of quality riding a horse through a garden in which two splendidly clothed women picnic beside a silver fountain, done in a very naïve style. I also bought sweets, dried fruits and cardamom, which is indispensable for making good tea.

I did some cooking with Bahram's mother, and she showed me how to make sweet rice in four different colours: *chahar rangūī*. The four colours are orange, the red of *serej*, the green of pistachios and the white of almonds.

I'll be spending the last few hours before leaving for the airport at the house of Davud and Fahimé, friends of Irene and Bahram whom I met in Barcelona, where they have bought an apartment in order to become Spanish residents. The idea wasn't to emigrate for good but to secure a foothold abroad in case things didn't work out at home. They have a lovely apartment in a luxurious building in north Tehrān. In the living room there are three carpets, each a work of art: one with small flowers repeated against a sky-blue background and surrounded by a broad ornamental border; one with a pink background; and the third covered with multicoloured flowers, in symmetrical groups, with a navy-blue shade predominating. Seeing these carpets after having admired so many in the course of my trip, I think: "Now *these* are the ones I'd really like to take away with me!" Davud and Fahimé are a very Iranian but also very modern couple: although they are wealthy, they are not ostentatious and obsessed with Western goods, as is often the case. They travel a great deal, because Davud is in charge of buying equipment for Iranian television. But what they tell you of their travel plans is no guide at all to when they will actually turn up in Barcelona, before disappearing again. At home we call them Mr and Mrs Lotto.

The tragedy of Davud and Fahimé's life, as they used to tell everyone, was that they didn't have children. Three years ago there were terrible floods in the north of Iran, where they have a house. There were many deaths, and many children lost their parents. They found a new-born baby girl in a basket at the door of their house, took her in as if she were the river's gift, and adopted her. Now they are happy.

Davud and Fahimé's cook prepared and served us a sumptuous meal, and afterwards we filled in the time before going to the airport listening to music and making tapes of the records I liked.

Irene and Toni Catany will stay here for a few days longer.

The plane home leaves at four in the morning. Irene, Bahram and Toni drop me off at the airport at two. The airport officials are not in a good mood. They are not friendly, like the ones we encountered on arriving, and they look like Revolutionary guards. They check all my bags and ask me if I am carrying money. Iranians fill their bags with food: sweets, pistachios, raisins, home-made preserves, the way the Spanish travel with sausages. The official talks so quickly that I can't understand what he's saying to me, and he doesn't want to repeat it, so I don't insist and slip through as best I can. The woman behind me is strictly dressed in a black *chādor*. Just as the inquisitive guard is about to open her bag, she distracts him by asking very humbly where she can find the praying area for women, because she wants to pray before embarking and doesn't know if she'll have time. Impressed by this devotion, the guard gives her careful directions, tells her she can close her bags, without even having looked at them or having asked her any questions, and wishes her well on her journey. I'm thinking: that's a good system for getting through customs in Islamic countries. Later, in the plane, I notice the same woman tucking into sweets from a box. Her head is uncovered, revealing hair dyed a yellowish blonde, and the change surprises me. But when we get off the plane, it is even more surprising: tight skirt, high-heeled shoes and bright red lipstick.

May

Barcelona

*I*RENE returned to Barcelona a couple of days later, and told me that Bubu wasn't going to get married after all, and that she and Rave would arrive in a few weeks. Which they did: they arrived and sat down at the foot of the first column they found in the area for incoming international visitors and transit passengers. Irene, who had gone to pick them up, had to argue with the guard on duty for a couple of hours before he would let her in to see if she could find them. She knew they had arrived, the plane had been showing as 'landed' for hours, and they still hadn't come out. But the guard said: "That's the regulation, Madame. You can't go through the gate unless you have a ticket and a passport."

Irene: "You go yourself then, please. It'll be easy to recognise them: one is an elderly Asian-looking woman, a grandmother, with almond-shaped eyes and a round face; the other is a young girl with Down's syndrome."

The guard: "With what?"

Irene: "Mongoloid, retarded, with narrow eyes and a very rounded face. Now please, if you would be kind enough to let me through or go and look for them yourself. They don't speak anything except Persian. This is the first time they've been out of their country, and they've been lost in there for hours."

Eventually her insistence prevailed and they let her in. She found Bubu and Rave straight away, sitting quietly on the floor at the foot of a column, with a look of eastern patience on their faces.

The problem then was how to get Bubu to her mother in Germany, and arrange for Rave to see various doctors to have all her medical problems checked out, before sending her off to her son in Sweden.

Rave had a visa for Sweden, but Bubu didn't have one for Germany. She would have to be smuggled across borders, in a car with Spanish number plates and unsuspicious-looking Spanish passengers, so that the guards wouldn't stop them to ask for their papers. I was happy to take Rave to the doctors, but not to take Bubu to Germany. Something was telling me no: deep down, I felt it was awfully wrong.

The transportation was organised with the help of some friends. Bubu was sedated with valium and put in the back seat of a rented car. They had no problems reaching their destination in a suburb of Hamburg, full of identical apartment blocks. On the seventeenth floor of one of these blocks, with everything from plants to donkeys on the landings, they found Nuri's flat, but she didn't come out to greet them until she had finished with the man who was in her room and sent him on his way. They were met at the door by her other child, a lad of twelve, bright as a button, they said, who was busy in the kitchen while his mother was working. And that's where they left Bubu.

Rave consulted practically every doctor in Barcelona, and finally ended up in Sweden.

I wasn't able to discover why the wedding hadn't gone ahead. There was no way to find out, because no-one would talk about it. I came to the conclusion that Bubu's opportunity had come too late. By that stage, some members of her family had managed to obtain visas for Australia, while others had arranged to move to Europe. Staying on to negotiate a marriage that mightn't have worked out anyway would have meant losing precious time and maybe missing the big chance. The castles I had been building in the air came crashing down, and I didn't want to find out more or ask for further explanations.

It wouldn't be true to say that because of this story of frustrated love, Iran has lost its magic for me. The simple fact that the wedding was a possibility, the way they talked about it, so gently and respectfully – these things are a reminder of the country's spirit. But I was saddened, because Iran is torn between two worlds, one advancing at the expense of the other. The way in which Bubu's fairy tale was cut short is just one of the consequences of this process, which nobody can hold back, however many Islamic revolutions break out.

Barcelona, 1995

*W*HAT became of Bubu? I ask about her each time I see a
member of the family, and they tell me she is well, and
has ceased to be a problem. Everything has fallen into place,
like the pieces of a puzzle, gradually assembled until they all
lock together. I don't know all the details, but from what I
have heard it seems that Bubu has already adapted to the
cramped cubicle that is her new home. No doubt there is a sofa
in front of the television, and that's where she spends her days,
watching moving pictures that often make her laugh. She's
probably still varnishing her nails and wearing necklaces of
coloured beads. When there's a knock on the door I imagine
she goes to welcome the men who come to visit her mother,
mainly Iranian men, regular clients, decent people, who go up
to the seventeenth floor of block number seventeen in an outer
suburb of Hamburg looking for a little warmth to melt their
frozen solitude. They probably chat with Bubu affectionately
while they are waiting and maybe bring her little gifts from
time to time. And her half-brother, who they say is bright as a
button, nearly fourteen now, can concentrate on the cooking
without being interrupted. He won't have to open the door
each time somebody knocks, and maybe he'll get to become a
doctor, which is what he wants to do. Perhaps, in the end,
Bubu has found her place in Germany: a place where she fits
in and feels useful.

I would like to be able to write to her or call her every now and then, but neither the telephone nor letters are much use with Bubu. A few days ago I was sitting in front of the television watching a news story about the severe cold spell affecting central Europe. I thought of her, and felt I had to send her a message. It was an impossible, symbolic message sent by someone performing a ceremony to comfort herself: I sent it via the television screen. After all, the angels must have their own communication system, no doubt using special channels to transmit their messages through space. I sat myself in front of the television, concentrated, and simply said "*Bubu, chekār mīkonī?*" How are things going, Bubu? I wrapped the message in warmth, to buoy it on its way, added a wink and blew it gently towards the screen, to help it to catch a wave. In a few seconds, those waves can cross the world. Bubu smiled and curled up on the sofa, making the most of the little bit of warmth I had sent her.

And Rave? Rave is in Sweden with her son. No doubt she's still surrounded by pots and pans, and even doing the shopping, having got used to the new streets and the new spaces, managing well, although she doesn't know the language. I imagine her cooking has created an Iranian enclave in Sweden, for the enjoyment of the whole family. Though she is accustomed to suffering in silence and putting on a brave face, her herpes must be hurting terribly and she is probably going blind, unless Swedish medicine has performed a miracle and stopped her suffering. One thing is certain: she won't be getting her daily ration of opium, but I think Rave is capable of giving up even that without a fuss, without a word, in silence. She may have a happy old age, reinvigorated by her new surroundings. I don't know if it's painful for her to be separated from Bubu – it must be – but in her patient eastern way, she probably thinks that Bubu is where she should be, according to Allah's plan, and accepts it serenely.

The phone must be busy between Stockholm and Hamburg; they'll be sending each other photos and videos, thinking of each other when they celebrate the feast days. During the long hours of the Swedish winter, when Rave is home alone she probably revisits scenes from her life: the vast snow-covered steppes around Tashkent, where she was born; the hide-covered yurts of her Mongolian tribe; hearing the din of horses trotting over the snow; remembering the first time she saw the clear eyes of her general, clearer by far than the waters of the Amu-Daria, the river she crossed with him at the outset of a long journey that took her over high mountains and finally to Tehrān. She must have been just seventeen. She also remembers her barnlike house on the outskirts of Tehrān, the way it gradually filled up with children, her chickens, her herbs, the visits of the general, old already and totally wasted; those years in Tehrān apartments, always cooking, always organising meals for the troops without complaining, trying not to make any noise, when there was nothing but noise all around her. Her sons and step-sons, her daughters and step-daughters, her sons-in-law and grandsons, with their various professions, an engineer, a plumber, a surveyor, a painter . . . scattered throughout the world. Most of all she remembers Bubu, her dear Bubu, with her warm, comforting body, the most faithful of them all, the one who, like herself, made no noise, just smiled when Rave rocked her to sleep or hugged her in her big motherly arms. The solitude of the immigrant – the immense solitude of the old immigrant – is like that of the prisoner serving a life sentence. The hatches close and you withdraw into the domain of your own memory, which becomes vast, a panoramic screen, while the outside world is just a series of formalities.

New York, 1996

A COUPLE of days ago, when I found out I was going to Chicago, I called Homa from Barcelona to say I would like to see her: I could stop off for a day in New York and we could meet. Since we parted in Tehrān so many years ago I have only received two letters from her. In the first, she told me she had got married, and in the second she gave me her address in New York, where she was living with her husband and son.

She suggested we meet at the Palace of the Moon at seven in the evening, on the day I had chosen.

"On Broadway?" I asked.

"No, in Queens, near where I live. We can be alone there, and it's a nice restaurant."

"Chinese, is it?"

"No, Cuban. Get a taxi and tell the driver to go down Flushing Meadows, and as soon as you turn into the avenue you'll see a neon sign in the gap between two tall buildings."

"A sign with pink and blue letters?"

"Yes. How did you know?" Without waiting for my answer, she went on: "You'll have to go round the block to get to the restaurant."

On the appointed day, without any more explicit instructions, I got into a taxi and headed for Queens. No sign of a pink and blue neon sign as we turned into Flushing Meadows.

It had been a cold winter day, and it was already completely dark; I could see myself getting lost in Queens searching for a Cuban restaurant with a Chinese-sounding name. Then, as the taxi stopped at the first set of lights, at the end of the cross-street, in the narrow gap between two tall buildings, I saw the neon letters spelling out 'Palace of the Moon'. Saved!

In the restaurant, I divested myself of coat, scarf, cap and gloves, and had already struck up a conversation in Spanish with the proprietor, who turned out to be a Chinese Cuban (though he called himself a Cuban Chinese), when Homa appeared with her long black hair loose and a mink coat that came down to her feet. Under the coat she was wearing a fine silk sleeveless dress. I was glad to see she had lost none of her boldness since our student days.

While we were eating she said to me: "I was in the rector's office when the scarf brigade came to demand that Manigé not be allowed to return to the college the following academic year. They were so determined it was frightening."

"Did they really have that much power then, those girls?" I asked.

"They certainly did," she replied. "They were followers of Ali Sharīatī, a professor in the School of Theology at the University of Tehrān, who set out to restore the dignity of Muslim women during the 1960s and '70s. When he died in 1976, many women were already following his lead, young students especially. It was a reaction to the way the identity of women was changing. Sharīatī drew on modern ideas about the equality of men and women. The scarf girls lent me a copy of his book *Fatima is Fatima*, in which he presents the wife of Ali, daughter of Mohammed and mother of Hussein and Hassan, as an exemplar of womanhood. For all Muslims, she is a saintly, perfect figure. She is innocent because she died young. She was generous and faithful, a good daughter, a devoted wife and educator of her children, but – and this was the tricky part – Sharīatī also showed her playing an active role in society and the Muslim community. He portrayed her participating in the struggles of her father and husband, demonstrating solidarity, especially with the poor, and protesting against injustice. Sharīatī provided a model of active femininity at a time when Iranian women were deeply disoriented. Girls from the middle classes and from poor families were integrated into the education system only to be cast adrift in a society with nothing to offer by way of role models but the stars of the movies, television and the glossy magazines: fictitious and unattainable models, imported from outside, asserting the supremacy of appearances. Sharīatī's alternative was a thinking, intelligent woman with a sense of mission and responsibility, struggling against injustice and on an equal footing with men."

"It sounds very attractive," I said. "I think even I would have volunteered to become an Iranian woman under those conditions."

"Well, it was attractive," she replied, "and realistic too. Something to replace the woman-as-Barbie-doll which had been the ideal until then. Sharīatī's followers took up the headscarf and the overgarment as a way of rejecting the dictates of sexist Western fashion, which only the privileged classes could afford. With a headscarf and an overgarment, women could go into offices, go to university and take part in demonstrations, like men, knowing their physical appearance wouldn't affect the way they related to society."

I interrupted her: "It sounds like you're saying it was a

blessing for Iranian women, but I've seen how that uniform is an obligation and there's simply no way of escaping it."

"That's the pity of it: the Revolution of 1979 made it obligatory, but I still think it allowed Iranian women from poor and disadvantaged backgrounds to acquire a certain autonomy with respect to men, and that was a good thing."

"You left pretty smartly yourself, though," I said. "Somehow, I just can't see you wearing a headscarf."

"Anajon," she said, using an affectionate form of address, "you know how I love silk dresses. I've been corrupted." She laughed. "Anyway, I'm not Iranian, even though I lived there for many years and married an Iranian man. I'm an Afghan, and as you know, Afghanistan is another world. We are nomads at heart, my friend. We grew up feeling tiny, between the vast earth and the immensity of the sky. There weren't so many of us –" She remained pensive for a moment, then shaking her head as if to snap out of a dream, she said: "Afghanistan is another story, more tragic than the story of Iran: people kill each other there and no-one even reports it. It's a forgotten country. The war has been going on for so long now that a whole generation of children and adolescents have learnt how to use weapons instead of learning how to read. That's all they can do. It's a ruined country. It always has been, in fact, back through the ages, since Chinggis Khaan went through leaving a wasteland behind him. Even before the most recent troubles, Afghanistan was a country without monuments, but, all the same, it was the last paradise. Iranians can go home, but we'll never be able to, though maybe one day our children will visit the country, along with tourists from North America, France or New Zealand. That's why Afghans who have emigrated to the developed world have a very different attitude from Iranians. We bring up our children to believe from the start that they belong to the new country and will take its nationality, and we do all we can to make sure they find their place without too much trauma, and have a positive attitude. For the rest of the world, Afghanistan doesn't exist. For us, it's just a memory without a future. None of our family is left there, not even distant relatives. You remember all those nights we spent talking about the history of Afghanistan with my father when you came to stay with us? Well, my father died, alone, three years ago. He didn't want to leave the country, and all his children were abroad. When he decided to stay, he knew he wouldn't see us again."

"What amazes me," I said to Homa, "is how people manage to adapt and get by when they are forced to emigrate, the way they make a go of it even in the most difficult circumstances. You're a prime example: you look so well and smart, you must be happy. Tell me about how you came to America."

"My husband and I came with our son, who was just nine months old. All we had were a few bulging suitcases and a little bit of money. The first day we set ourselves up in a poky little flat some Iranian friends in New York had found for us. The second day, I went down to the local print shop, carrying my little boy, to get some flyers made up offering my services for sewing, mending and dressmaking. You know how much I've always liked sewing. I put them in every letterbox in the neighbourhood; I left them in shops, stuck them on the walls of the subway, gave them out in the street. On the third day I got a call from a grandmother who couldn't manage to thread the needle to finish off a dress she was making for herself. And that's how my American adventure started. I let my university studies go. I felt it was better to get straight to work sewing for people in the neighbourhood than to go in search of a professional job. As soon as I could, I bought a second-hand sewing machine and started building up my clientele: I did hems, changed zips, and from time to time I got an order for a dress. I worked at home, so I was able to look after my boy. Women began to realise I had good dress sense, and that they looked prettier when they took my advice. After a while I started to work mostly for Iranian clients: I know what they like and how they think. Now I dress practically the whole of New York's Iranian community. I've set up a workshop with a retail outlet, and women who want a dress made meet me there by appointment. It has to be done by appointment to avoid embarrassing encounters, because they all know each other and go to the same weddings and parties. I have become a counsellor: I help them to choose the cloth, the cut and even the jewellery they should wear for each occasion. In strict confidence of course. You see, Anajon, it all took less than ten years. It was much harder for my husband to find work. And one day, when we've got more time, we'll talk about Afghanistan."

"And what happened in the rector's office?" I asked her.

"The scarf brigade talked about the books in Manigé's room, her behaviour with boys, and her past; they said she was a bad example for the other girls in the college. And people were talking about her at the university, which was bound to give the college a bad name. Then they summoned Manigé, who came in tying up her dressing gown, with her hair all in a mess. She found herself caught between the group of fundamentalists wrapped in their drab garments, staring at her menacingly from one corner of the office like the chorus of a Greek tragedy, and the rector with her Chanel suit and Cartier watch, beautiful, cultured and prepossessing, smiling hypocritically as if nothing was wrong. On one side, the image of what was to come; on the other, the image of what would disappear; and at that moment, there was no place for Manigé on either side. In the heady days of the Shāh, in that rich and corrupt society, a girl like her, intelligent and street-smart as well, with excellent academic qualifications, would have been able to get ahead. But by this stage, the regime was already tottering. There were signs: you saw them, and so did I. In the new Islamic society, it would have been very hard for Manigé. Nobody would have helped her to get out of the country: her family, who were poor and uneducated, had disowned her; and even the most progressive political parties and groups had trouble coping with the fact that she had been raped and was sexually uninhibited. The rector told her that she was considering the possibility of not letting her return the following academic year, and when she began to explain and justify herself, Manigé walked out of the office in a fury, slamming the door. We followed her out, but all we saw was the door to the terrace left open."

I looked into Homa's eyes and saw that they were glistening. I didn't want to keep talking about it, and I guess she didn't either, because the next thing she said to me was: "You remember the day you almost killed me for laughing at that Beatles song you used to love?"

"I certainly do, and I still curse you every time I hear it," I answered, joking.

"You know I think of you every time my son puts that CD on. And then I remember walking around the bazaar in Tehrān with you, studying together in the room, our strolls in Farah Park, and I always remember Dr Butterfly and the yellow pansy he wore in his buttonhole. By the way, I thought I saw him driving a taxi in Manhattan the other day, the same white sideburns, the same nose . . . but by the time I got across the street to see if he was wearing the pansy, which would have been proof positive, he had disappeared in his taxi. It must have been a hallucination, because an ex-professor from the University of Tehrān who lives near me, and who knew him, told me a little while ago that he had fallen in love with a woman of ill repute in Germany, and had gone to live with her in Australia."

"You're kidding! I'm glad though, because I was starting to fear the worst. He came to see me in Barcelona a couple of times when he was living in Germany, and wrote occasionally, but it's been years since I've had news. The last time I saw him, he seemed sad. Maybe he's finally found someone who loves him."

"I don't know if he'll find pansies in Australia," said Homa, before falling into a thoughtful silence.

"Homa, I still remember the day you came to the college for the first time. I had already been living in the room for a week when you appeared. The first thing you did was to open your suitcase and take out a prayer mat and a white veil. You put the mat on the floor – and I was thinking: how is she going to know which way Mecca is? – then immediately covered yourself with the veil, which came down to your feet, and started to pray, bowing deeply. That was the only time I ever saw you pray."

"That's right, I didn't feel I needed to after that. Our room was like a little chapel; we were in perfect harmony with nature, and everything we did was part of an ongoing prayer."

Homa fell silent again, as if suspended in a dream. Eventually, she said: "Do you realise, Anajon, that in a month it'll be Nō Rūz again? The roses will come into flower in the gardens of Golestān, and everything will smell of spring."

And then, as if somewhere within both of us a switch had been thrown, we began to recite the first Persian poem we had learnt by heart in Dr Sūtūdeh's class:

> *The spring reveals a patch of earth*
> *that seems a morsel in the jaws of the snow . . .*

And we ended up filling the restaurant with laughter.

Barcelona, April 1996

$\mathcal{I}$RENE has just rung me from Chicago, where she now lives, and she told me that Bubu, Nuri and Rave have gone to live in Australia.

"Australia? You're kidding! How did they manage that?"

"I've got no idea, but you know those Iranians, they have all sorts of tricks up their sleeves. And apparently Nuri has got married too."

"Married? Who to?"

"Some Iranian professor who used to go and see her from time to time, you know. They say he's elegant and cultivated. They're so serious, aren't they?" I can hear her laughter clear as crystal down the telephone line.

"Irene, I think I might know this professor you're talking about."

"You know him? How come?"

"Is he called Sherzad?"

"Yes, I think that's the name they said, yes . . ."

"It must be him then. He was a professor at the University of Tehrān when I was studying there. My roommate Homa – I'm sure I've told you about Homa – anyway, she and I used to call him Dr Butterfly, because he was always spectacularly dressed: he had sideburns like Burt Lancaster in *The Leopard*, and always wore a pansy in his buttonhole. When I was in New York, Homa told me that he had gone to live in Australia.

He was one of the university's great characters. Later, when the Revolution started, he went to live in Germany. That's where he was teaching the last time he came to see me in Barcelona. He was a good friend, though I'd sometimes go for years without hearing from him. I'm glad, I'm really glad. Dr Butterfly never told me about his family. He was a solitary, sensitive, delicate sort of man. His manner was pleasant and discreet, and he always spoke quietly. Given his personality, I could never quite understand why he put on such a grand show, buying himself flashy cars and sophisticated clothes, bordering on the extravagant. That was his link to the Shāh's Persia, the Persia of the 2500th anniversary. But deep down, Dr Sherzad belonged to the Persian heartland: he was humble, gentle and wise."

So many things you could never predict, I thought as I hung up. And then a moment later I realised that Bubu and Rave would be together again, and that with the new arrangement the dark cloud that appeared in my mind each time I thought of them had gone.

Sometimes, in forbidding circumstances, people with handicaps manage to achieve things that seem impossible. So far, in two years, Bubu has travelled halfway round the world. And celebrated Nō Rūz once again with her grandmother, her mother, her uncles, aunts and cousins, in a country where the sun is strong, like in Iran. Maybe she even has a father now.

Life goes on, and if I don't finish this book here, I never will.

BIBLIOGRAPHY

V. S. Naipaul, *Among the Believers*, Deutch, London.

Mark Kravetz, *Irano Nox*, Grasset, Paris.

Yann Richard et al, *Téhéran*, Autrement, Serie Monde n 27, Paris.

Czeslaw Milosz, *El pensamiento cautivo*, Tusquets, Barcelona.

Forough Hekmat, *The Art of Persian Cooking*, Ebn-e-sina, Tehrān.

Pierre Loti, *Vers Ispahan,* Société de publications d'ouvrages classiques sur l'Iran, Tehrān.

Lily Litvak, *Viaje al interior de Persia, El itinerario de Rivadeneyra (1874–1875),* Ed. del Serbal, Barcelona.

M. A. Boisard, *L'Islam aujourd'hui*, Unesco, Paris 1984.

Eshan Naraghi, *Enseignement et changements sociaux en Iran*, Editions de la Maison des Sciences de l'Homme, Paris 1992.

LONELY PLANET JOURNEYS

JOURNEYS is a unique collection of travel writing – published by the company that understands travel better than anyone else.

It is a series for anyone who has ever experienced – or dreamed of – the magical moment when they encountered a strange culture or saw a place for the first time. They are tales to read while you're planning a trip, while you're on the road or while you're in an armchair, in front of a fire.

These outstanding titles explore our planet through the eyes of a diverse group of international writers. JOURNEYS books catch the spirit of a place, illuminate a culture, recount an adventure, or introduce a fascinating way of life. They always entertain, and always enrich the experience of travel.

'Lively, intelligent and varied . . . an important contribution to travel literature' – *Age (Melbourne)*

LONELY PLANET UNPACKED
Travel Disaster Stories
By Tony Wheeler and other Lonely Planet Writers

Every traveller has a horror story to tell: lost luggage, bad weather, illness or worse. In this lively collection of travel disaster tales, Lonely Planet writers share their worst moments of life on the road.

From Kenya to Sri Lanka, from Brazil to Finland, from the Australian outback to India, these travellers encounter hurri-canes, road accidents, secret police and nasty parasites. Reading these funny and frightening stories from the dark side of the road will make you think twice about a career as a travel writer!

'Lonely Planet celebrates its road-stained wretches in . . . a collection of tales of delightful disaster' – *Don George, Travel Editor, salon.com*

MALI BLUES
Traveling to an African Beat
Lieve Joris
(translated by Sam Garrett)

Drought, rebel uprisings, ethnic conflict: these are the predominant images of West Africa. But as Lieve Joris travels in Senegal, Mauritania and Mali, she meets survivors, fascinating individuals charting new ways of living between tradition and modernity. With her remarkable gift for drawing out people's stories, Joris brilliantly captures the rhythms of a world that refuses to give in.

THE GATES OF DAMASCUS
Lieve Joris
(translated by Sam Garrett)

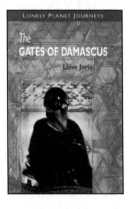

This best-selling book is a beautifully drawn portrait of day-to-day life in modern Syria. Through her intimate contact with local people, Lieve Joris draws us into the fascinating world that lies behind the gates of Damascus. Hala's husband is a political prisoner, jailed for his opposition to the Assad regime; through the author's friendship with Hala we see how Syrian politics impacts on the lives of ordinary people.

'she has expanded the boundaries of travel writing'
– Times Literary Supplement

KINGDOM OF THE FILM STARS
Journey into Jordan
Annie Caulfield

Kingdom of the Film Stars is a travel book and a love story. With honesty and humour, Annie Caulfield writes of travelling in Jordan and falling in love with a Bedouin with film-star looks.

She offers fascinating insights into the country – from the tent life of traditional women to the hustle of downtown Amman – and unpicks tight-woven Western myths about the Arab world.

'part travelogue, part love story – and always compelling'
– Mademoiselle

THE OLIVE GROVE
Travels in Greece
Katherine Kizilos

Katherine Kizilos travels to fabled islands, troubled border zones and her family's village deep in the mountains. She vividly evokes breathtaking landscapes, generous people and passionate politics, capturing the complexities of a country she loves.

The Olive Grove tells of other journeys too: the life-changing journey made by the author's emigrant father; the migration of young Greeks to cities; and the tremendous impact of tourism on Greek society.

'beautifully captures the real tensions of Greece'
– Sunday Times

THE LONELY PLANET STORY

Lonely Planet published its first book in 1973 in response to the numerous 'How did you do it?' questions Maureen and Tony Wheeler were asked after driving, busing, hitching, sailing and railing their way from England to Australia.

Written at a kitchen table and hand collated, trimmed and stapled, *Across Asia on the Cheap* became an instant local bestseller, inspiring thoughts of another book.

Eighteen months in South-East Asia resulted in their second guide, *South-East Asia on a shoestring*, which they put together in a backstreet Chinese hotel in Singapore in 1975. The 'yellow bible', as it quickly became known to backpackers around the world, soon became *the* guide to the region. It has sold well over half a million copies and is now in its 10th edition, still retaining its familiar yellow cover.

Today there are over 350 titles, including travel guides, walking guides, language kits and phrasebooks, travel atlases and travel literature. The company is the largest independent travel publisher in the world.

The emphasis continues to be on travel for independent travellers. Tony and Maureen still travel for several months of each year and play an active part in the writing, updating and quality control of Lonely Planet's guides.

They have been joined by over 80 authors and 400 staff at our offices in Melbourne (Australia), Oakland (USA), London (UK) and Paris (France). Travellers themselves also make a valuable contribution to the guides through the feedback we receive in thousands of letters each year and on our web site.

The people at Lonely Planet strongly believe that travellers can make a positive contribution to the countries they visit, both through their appreciation of the countries' culture, wildlife and natural features, and through the money they spend. In addition, the company makes a direct contribution to the countries and regions it covers. Since 1986 a percentage of the income from each book has been donated to ventures such as famine relief in Africa; aid projects in India; agricultural projects in Central America; Greenpeace's efforts to halt French nuclear testing in the Pacific; and Amnesty International.

'I hope we send people out with the right attitude about travel. You realise when you travel that there are so many different perspectives about the world, so we hope these books will make people more interested in what they see.'
                                                              – Tony Wheeler